THE RUABON TO BARMOUTH LINE

THE RUABON TO BARMOUTH LINE

THE RUABON TO BALA SECTION

PETER DICKINSON

By the 1960s, the station of Berwyn to the west of Llangollen had been downgraded to an unstaffed halt, with only a small wooden hut providing protection for the few passengers still using it. Yet, a century earlier, an impressive station had been constructed to suit the needs of the landed gentry, including the railway's first chairman and a much-celebrated German-British locomotive designer. It is refreshing to see that the lineside is still immaculately kept in this 1963 view, much to the credit of the local Permanent Way gang.

Fonthill Media Language Policy

Fonthill Media publishes in the international English language market. One language edition is published worldwide. As there are minor differences in spelling and presentation, especially with regard to American English and British English, a policy is necessary to define which form of English to use. The Fonthill Policy is to use the form of English native to the author. Peter Dickinson was born and educated in Merseyside; therefore, British English has been adopted in this publication.

Fonthill Media Limited
Fonthill Media LLC
www.fonthillmedia.com
office@fonthillmedia.com

First published in the United Kingdom and the United States of America 2019

British Library Cataloguing in Publication Data:
A catalogue record for this book is available from the British Library

Copyright © Peter Dickinson 2019

ISBN 978-1-78155-214-8

The right of Peter Dickinson to be identified as the author of this work has been asserted by him in accordance with the Copyright, Designs and Patents Act 1988.

All rights reserved. No part of this publication may be reproduced, stored in a retrieval system or transmitted in any form or by any means, electronic, mechanical, photocopying, recording or otherwise, without prior permission in writing from Fonthill Media Limited

Typeset in 10.5pt on 13pt Sabon
Printed and bound in England

Foreword

For many, there is a tangible yet unexplainable sense of misty-eyed romanticism when mention is made of a long-lost railway line. This is particularly acute for lines where it is still possible to travel along at least one section of it, as part of the UK's fine portfolio of preserved heritage railways on board a steam-hauled train.

The great British countryside is littered with all the traces and clues to indicate the former presence of a railway line: that suspiciously straight stretch of hedging cutting across fields, the seemingly pointless bridges crossing wild oblivion, or even those overgrown narrow embankments now populated with large encroaching trees.

While identifying a former railway line is one thing, it is quite another to determine where it went and why it was even built in the first place. Who used the line? What purpose did it serve? What stories does it have to tell?

A prime example of such a long-lost railway is the former cross-country route between the village of Ruabon at its eastern end and the seaside town of Barmouth in the west. In its heyday, a journey of over 50 miles along the line was officially described by the Great Western Railway as being 'a paradise for artists and fisherman and a country rich in mountain streams, wild woods and wide far views, unbeaten in any part of Wales'.

A 10-mile stretch of the line between the towns of Llangollen and Corwen still exists and has been lovingly restored back to its former glory thanks to the efforts of the volunteers and staff of the preserved Llangollen Railway. Further down the valley, a 4.5-mile stretch along the shoreline of Llyn Tegid can still be sampled from the comfort of a railway carriage on board one of the Bala Lake Railway's narrow-gauge trains.

However, for the most part, the route of the Ruabon to Barmouth line has passed back into the hands of Mother Nature. Many sections of the trackbed have been sold off in piecemeal fashion to farmers or other individuals, while in some cases, the route has been completely erased by encroaching housing and infrastructure developments.

Unlike many authors of railway publications covering a variety of aspects of the line's history, I am not of the age to remember the Ruabon to Barmouth line in operation during those so-called 'Golden Days of Steam'. My first encounter with the line came during a six-week-long university field trip studying the geology of the Dee Valley back in 2011. The western part of my field area encompassed (somewhat fortuitously) the preserved Llangollen Railway between its Llangollen and Berwyn stations. Indeed, it soon became possible for me to tell the time of day simply by the progress and distant whistling of the steam trains as they echoed along the valley.

By contrast, the eastern area encompassed part of the old line between Llangollen and the former Sun Bank Halt. Once outside of the town and the associated decimation that Llangollen has inflicted upon the trackbed in the years since its closure, the route of the old railway appears to lead triumphantly eastwards and is particularly easy to trace. It was this poignant reminder of a seemingly lost age that sparked my desire to further investigate the line's history.

To celebrate the 150th anniversary of the Llangollen and Corwen Railway (more on this later, but in short, the second section of the route to be built), I published a short book *Steam in the Dee Valley*. This charted the full, albeit brief, history of the route between Ruabon and one of the bigger intermediate stations in the town of Corwen. However, it was (in the broadest sense possible) a traditional railway history publication focusing mainly on the key dates and railway infrastructure.

This book aims to take you on a voyage of exploration and discovery that will give a fuller picture of the valley the railway served, the characters involved, and the reasons why it was built where it was in the first place. It is arranged to start at Ruabon (the main junction station from where the majority of services over the line commenced) and proceeds westwards as far as the lakeside town of Bala. I wanted to show how the railway fitted into the landscape and how the communities it served were changed by its coming.

Inevitably, there are omissions and I look forward to hearing from people who have stories to tell or who simply wish to point out where I have gone wrong—I am sure there will be many places. A second volume covering the route from Bala to Barmouth is now in preparation and I would be grateful for any additional views or information for inclusion in it. I must add my dedication to my long-suffering partner Leodina, who has endured losing the dining room table to my paperwork and research for a considerable number of months while preparing this book.

The book is illustrated throughout with many previously unpublished historical photographs but be warned—if it is yet another photographic album of steam-hauled trains in the 1950s and 1960s you are after, do look elsewhere. If this is not the case (and I truly hope it is not), please take this as the green flag and guard's whistle for us to proceed.

Peter Dickinson
Bromsgrove, 2019

Contents

Foreword — 5

1. Rails into the Dee Valley — 9
2. Onwards to Corwen and Bala — 21
3. Ruabon to Llangollen — 30
4. Llangollen to Corwen — 69
5. Corwen to Bala Junction — 100
6. Railway Fundamentals — 130
7. Tourism — 138
8. Moving the Goods — 144

Bibliography — 159

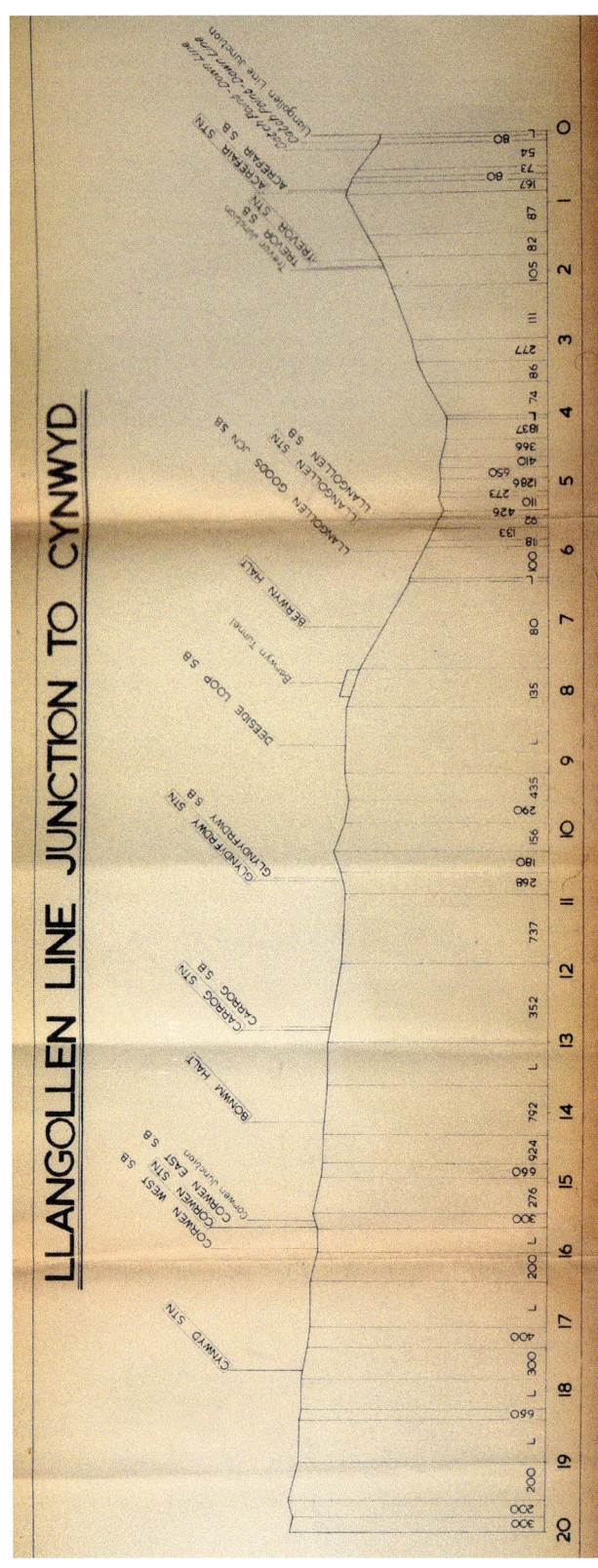

Gradient profile.

1
Rails into the Dee Valley

Conventional reasoning would dictate that the logical place to start a history of the Ruabon to Barmouth line would, of course, be Ruabon. Yet, for reasons that will soon become clear, this account actually starts on another railway line about 3 miles to the south at a point along the modern A5 road between Ruabon and Chirk. This site today is occupied by a builders' merchant but was once an important railhead for the Dee Valley.

In October 1848, the Shrewsbury and Chester Railway opened its route between Shrewsbury and Ruabon. A station called 'Llangollen Road' was opened 1 mile to the north of Chirk and was located on the south side of the Thomas Telford's London and Holyhead road (later to become the A5). Connecting road coaches ran the 5.25 miles between the station and the town of Llangollen, which was even being shown in the railway timetables.

Through ticketing was available from Llangollen using the road and rail services, with the price of a second-class ticket to Shrewsbury around 33 miles away costing 3 shillings and 8 pence in 1850. By contrast, a second-class ticket to Chester around 25 miles away cost 3 shillings and 3 pence.

Llangollen Road station was listed in the Bradshaw's descriptive railway handbook of Great Britain and Ireland in 1861. Bradshaw was keen to extoll the virtues of the Dee Valley, noting of Llangollen Road:

> The station is most admirably situated for parties desirous of visiting the finest scenery in North Wales, as coaches are generally in attendance to meet each train, to convey passengers to the principal places in the vicinity. The drive on the great Holyhead road from this station cannot be surpassed for beauty in the kingdom. It traverses the whole length of the Vale of Llangollen and the valley of the Dee up to Corwen—every turn of the road presenting the most beautiful scenery.

> The Vale of Llangollen is said to equal any of the beauties of the Rhine and it no doubt surpasses them in works of art, the aqueduct and viaduct being splendid ornaments to this lovely work of nature.

Despite the station's remote location away from major towns and villages, Llangollen Road benefitted from an intensive passenger service between Shrewsbury and Chester. The March 1850 timetable showed that seven trains ran in each direction Monday to Friday, with two trains each way on Sundays.

The demise of Llangollen Road was to come in June 1862, when a new railway was built between Ruabon and Llangollen. As the town could now be reached by train, there was no longer a need for Llangollen Road as a passenger station and it closed its doors on 1 July 1862. The original station building still survives as a private dwelling today.

However, that was not to be the end of the story, as 'Llangollen Road' was destined to reappear in the public timetables in the following century. On 1 October 1905, the Great Western Railway opened a halt on the northern side of the Holyhead Road, which was initially called 'Llangollen Road'. This swansong for the name was only to last seven months, with a renaming to Whitehurst Halt taking place on 1 May the following year. This too has since been consigned to history, with the final closure of the halt coming in September 1960.

Now often dismissed, the original Llangollen Road station had a substantial role to play in the history of railways through the Dee Valley. In modern parlance, it was the Victorian equivalent of a 'Parkway' station and would have given many locals their first taste of rail travel.

A little way along the tracks to the north of the old Llangollen Road station, we find a grand and impressive piece of railway infrastructure that defiantly stamps the railway firmly into the landscape. When a line between Shrewsbury and Chester was being proposed, the broad river valley of the River Dee posed a major challenge to the Victorian railway builders.

Their solution was to construct the Cefn Viaduct, which today has nineteen stone arches each with a span of 60 feet. The viaduct measures 1,508 feet long and 147 feet high. The ceremony of keying the last stone of the viaduct was performed by Mr W. Ormsby Gore, the chairman of the Shrewsbury and Chester Railway on 14 August 1848. In the following speeches, he went on to say that the viaduct's opening was an 'extraordinary triumph of art over the difficulties of nature'.

While the scale and design of the viaduct certainly warranted the fanfare, the fact that it took just two years to complete makes it even more impressive. What was instrumental in achieving this fast pace of construction was the nearby canal system, enabling the shipment of sandstone from the quarries of Cefn Mawr on the northern side of the Dee Valley, across the Pontcysyllte Aqueduct to the southern side. The canal's benefit at the time was soon to be short-lived, with the new railway network destined to take over the mantle as the dominant transporter of goods in the area.

The mastermind behind the Cefn Viaduct was a young Scottish engineer who was initially more at home with rocks under the ground than those being suspended high above it. Coming from a very modest background, he was to become the fundamental figure in the building of the future Ruabon to Barmouth railway. His name was Henry Robertson.

Robertson: Profile of the Man

Henry Robertson was born in Banff, Scotland, in January 1816 and was the youngest of eight children. His parents were Scottish through and through and he always spoke of himself as being a Celt of the Celts. Robertson was originally intended for the Ministry but feeling he had no real calling for it, he wisely decided to look at professions more suited to his interests and abilities.

An old friend, who knew the family in Banff, spoke of them as being more 'noted for their literary and artistic gifts' than for their business acumen. Robertson, however, turned out to be an exception. Besides being a brilliant scholar, he proved himself to have a good head for business.

After receiving his early education in the schools of his native town, he was accepted into Aberdeen University where he graduated with an MA before he was twenty. Robertson found work as a mining engineer and worked down collieries in Lanarkshire, often commenting that for months in the year he never saw the sun except on a Sunday.

His efforts to start a colliery of his own were quickly thwarted by the local landowner on the grounds that he was far too young. Around the same time, the first great railway boom was taking place, with many new lines springing up right across the UK. Robertson became a pupil of two big names in railway engineering: Robert Stephenson (of the Rainhill Trials and 'Rocket' fame) and Joseph Locke. Among other works, he was tasked was the actual levelling and setting out parts of the challenging West Coast route over Shap.

Robertson was destined to have many fortunate escapes from death over his life and the first occurred during this time. Having heard that one of the very first steam-powered cars was working the Edinburgh district, Robertson decided to go and see it for himself. The horse-drawn coach in which he was travelling was delayed and when he arrived, he found the steam car had already gone about 1 mile down the road and he could not catch it up. It had only travelled a little bit further when the boiler exploded, killing everyone on board. The incident brought home just how dangerous and unpredictable the early steam-powered vehicles could be.

During the late 1830s, Robertson schemed and built the new Dundee Waterworks, where for the second time he nearly lost his life. While overseeing the works, Robertson found himself trapped in an underground reservoir filling with water and if he had not dived under the apron of the trap, he would have perished.

A slack period in the great railway boom enabled Robertson to broaden his sights and gained some very valuable experience building skew arches and bridges. He applied for, and obtained, a contract to construct the overhead bridges on the

Glasgow and Greenock railway, which was then being built. Robertson made his first real profit on the works, but it also gave him much experience in dealing with contractors on the larger works he carried out.

However, it was to be Robertson's skills at dancing that would give him his next big break. Robertson was a keen athlete, exceedingly nimble on his feet and these attracted the attention of a Mr Matthieson at a party in Glasgow. Matthieson was a very successful contractor and a man of great influence within the city. Robertson must have made quite an impression as he was offered a job there and then, taking up a position on Matthieson's team.

It so happened that one of the Scottish banks had advanced considerable sums of money for the development of the mineral district in North Wales. Matthieson was approached to create an independent report on the proposed investments and asked if he could recommend a young engineer who would undertake the job. Matthieson at once recommended Robertson, who found himself being dispatched to the Welsh village of Brymbo, in the hills to the west of Wrexham.

The rocks in this area of North-East Wales were found to contain a wide range of useful resources which were of great industrial importance. Coal had been dug out of the ground in Brymbo since the late 1400s, but this had really only been on a small scale before the start of the 1800s. The seams were found to yield different types of coal: including steam, house, gas and coking coals, as well as a variety known as cannel coal, which would latterly be used to produce oil.

Coal was by no means the only useful commodity in the area. Iron ore proved to be a very important find, while clays were used for making terracotta and bricks. Limestone quarried from the hills was found to be particularly suited for cement making, while the local sandstone was useful as moulding sand in steelworks. The silica found within certain parts of the sandstone was also useful in the making of china and earthenware goods, while metal mines extracting both lead and zinc were also opening up in the region.

With all the relevant natural resources in abundance, an ironworks had been established in Brymbo long before Robertson first visited the area. A gentleman by the name of John Wilkinson, an ironmaster from nearby Bersham, had bought the Brymbo Estate in 1792 and four years later established his new ironworks. In its first year, it produced 884 tons of iron and this seemed to fuel Wilkinson's ambitions for the site, with a new blast furnace being added in 1804.

However, after Wilkinson's death in 1808, the ironworks suffered from legal disputes, the absence of a skilled ironmaster and a slump in orders after the end of the Napoleonic Wars. The ironworks were finally sold in 1829 (in the very same year that the famous Rainhill Trials were being held further north) and were destined to remain idle for the next decade.

Robertson's arrival in 1842 was to herald a new era, not just for the Brymbo ironworks, but for the entire area too. At its heart would be Britain's growing railway network.

Railway Mania

It had become evident to Robertson that the prosperity and profitability of Brymbo were constrained by how effectively the finished products could be transported to customers. By the early 1840s, there was a growing need for a railway to serve the area. Robertson had already had first-hand experience with railway building and could see the advantages they could bring.

The growing railway network had not yet extended its tentacles deep into north-east Wales but was closing in with great speed. Railways linking the historic Roman city of Chester with Birkenhead to the north and Crewe to the east were opened in 1840. A proposed scheme to build a railway between Chester and Holyhead via the North Wales coast gained Parliamentary approval in 1844 and proved to be a catalyst for many other similar schemes.

Encouraged by directors of the proposed Chester and Holyhead Railway, the locally promoted North Wales Mineral Railway Company was set up in 1844 with Robertson proving to be a key player. The line would leave the Chester and Holyhead Railway's metals on the outskirts of Chester before striking southwards to the mining town of Wrexham.

Parliamentary approval to construct the North Wales Mineral Railway and its extension to Ruabon was gained in 1844. The Act of Parliament for the line south of the Dee called the Shrewsbury, Oswestry and Chester Junction Railway was obtained in 1845, with the Act amalgamating these two sections being obtained in 1846. These two lengths of railway were arguably the most troublesome of any that Robertson undertook, not only due to the major engineering work required, but also due to the opposition the Acts of Parliament had received. Indeed, it was necessary at times to do some of the survey work for the new railway under the cover of darkness. Much of this opposition arose from the fear of Wrexham-mined coal being transported to the south side of the River Dee, where it would be in direct competition with coal being mined there.

However, despite all the opposition, the new railway opened from Chester to Ruabon in 1846, complete with a dedicated freight-only line branching off near Wrexham to serve the area around Brymbo. Robertson was then faced with the prospect of crossing over the Dee Valley to the south of Ruabon, connecting with the new tracks already being laid northwards from Shrewsbury.

He had already drawn up plans for a grand viaduct to span the Dee Valley, but no contractor could be found who would undertake the job. It looked as if his plans for the through route would be held up indefinitely, but fate seemed to be on Robertson's side.

One day, Robertson was standing on the platform at Wrexham, talking to the station master while waiting for his train to depart for Chester, when he noticed a stranger getting on board. He asked the station master who the gentleman was, to be told 'Oh that is Mr Brassey, the great Railway Contractor'. 'Hold the train!' came Robertson's response as he darted back into the station's booking office to collect his plans for the new viaduct. Having got them, Robertson jumped into the same compartment on the train that Brassey was in, introduced himself and by the time the train had arrived in Chester, Brassey had agreed to build the viaduct.

This chance encounter marked the beginning of a life-long friendship between the two men, with them going on to construct many miles of railway together—Robertson overseeing the engineering and Brassey the contracting. The viaduct took about two years to build and the first public trains over the structure (and its nearby counterpart, the Cefn Viaduct) commenced in 1848.

During construction of the Shrewsbury to Chester route, plans were already being drawn up for railways along the Dee Valley, either as branch lines to Llangollen or as part of a cross-country route serving the Welsh coast. The great 'Railway Mania' of 1845–46 spawned an astonishing number of railway projects all seeking financial backing, with some being hare-brained even by today's standards.

In 1845, the London and Holyhead Direct Railway proposed an atmospheric railway going by way of Banbury, Stratford-upon-Avon, Kidderminster, and Bridgnorth to Shrewsbury where it would have joined the Shrewsbury, Oswestry and Chester Junction Railway, before diverting off via the Vale of Llangollen and the Holyhead Road (A5) through Capel Curig. A similar scheme by the Grand London and Dublin Approximation planned for an atmospheric railway following the same route as the London and Holyhead Direct north of Banbury, except that it took the Nant Ffrancon Pass to Bangor. Neither scheme was ultimately pursued.

Instead of using steam locomotives, trains on these atmospheric railways would have moved by a system of atmospheric (vacuum) traction propelling them along. A piston attached to the train would have been contained in a large metal tube laid between the tracks. Prior to the train leaving, the air was pumped out of the pipe ahead of the train, while air at atmospheric pressure was admitted to the pipe behind the piston, propelling the train forward. The system was unsuccessfully trialled during the 1840s, with the most notable section being Brunel's South Devon Railway between Exeter and Newton Abbot. Likewise, neither the London and Holyhead Direct nor the Grand London and Dublin Approximation railway schemes were ultimately pursued.

Financial depression followed the first great 'Railway Mania', although, in 1847, schemes were drawn up for a Birkenhead and Llangollen Railway and a Shrewsbury and Chester Railway Llangollen branch. The bills for these were presented for debate before Parliament but both were withdrawn. In November 1853, a Denbighshire Railway scheme briefly appeared, involving a route from Ruabon to Rhyl via Llangollen, Corwen, and Ruthin.

The Public Meeting

On completion of the railway between Shrewsbury and Chester in 1848, there had been much talk of connecting Llangollen in with it. Various schemes were mooted, plans prepared, and suggestions made, but nothing had happened. The whole railway problem was becoming something of a sore point among the disappointed townsfolk.

To rub salt into the wounds, the nearby town of Ruabon was already prospering from its new-found position on the railway network. The first station there had been fairly small, with only two platforms and a goods yard on one side. Its station building was designed by the architect Thomas Penson in an Italianate style and greeted its first passengers in 1846.

When the line south from Ruabon (via the new Dee and Cefn Viaducts) opened to a new temporary station at Shrewsbury two years later, Ruabon's brief role as a terminus meant that an engine shed and turntable had already been constructed there. The shed was closed when the Shrewsbury and Chester Railway was absorbed into the expanding Great Western Railway in 1854 but appears to have remained in use as a locomotive stabling point for some years afterwards. The turntable was also retained and was later replaced by a much larger version on the opposite side of the line.

The coming of the railway to Ruabon had brought with it new job opportunities, investment and a connection with important trade centres, providing new markets for the local colliery owners. By comparison, Llangollen was still very much a 'poor town'. Very few houses in the town had a supply of piped water or any sort of satisfactory sewage disposal. The arrival of Thomas Telford's London to Holyhead road (now the A5) and the construction of a canal had begun to regenerate Llangollen, with an influx of visitors beginning to increase the town's size and importance.

Yet, it was to be a full decade later that a true glimmer of hope was to first appear. On 16 October 1858, a public meeting was held in Llangollen's County Hall to discuss the viability of connecting the town with the rest of the railway network and the route any such new line should take.

As can be imagined, the meeting caused a lot of interest in the weeks leading up to it and a large number of interested and influential people were in attendance. Colonel R. Middleton Biddulph of Chirk Castle, who was at the time the lord lieutenant of Denbighshire, was elected to chair the meeting and immediately carried the first resolution of the meeting: 'That the construction of a railway to Llangollen would be a great public advantage and is deserving of the support of the town and neighbourhood'.

It was unsurprising that this was accepted without serious question, given that the townsfolk were being represented by the great and good of the area. Among those in attendance in the room were: Major (later Colonel) Tottenham of Plas Rhysgog, Berwyn; T. E. Dickin of Black Park, Chirk; G. H. Whalley of Plas Madoc, Ruabon (Member of Parliament for Peterborough); Robert Piercy (chief engineer of the New British Iron Company, Acrefair); Richard Ellerton of Bryn Tysilio, Berwyn (founder of the Vivod Estate and one of the first directors of the Brymbo steelworks); William Henry Darby of Brymbo (manager of Brymbo steelworks); Captain Burkinson (representing Sir Watkin Williams-Wynn); Rev. William Edwards (vicar of Llangollen and the father of Dr Alfred G. Edwards, the first Archbishop of Wales); Ebenezer Cooper (a well-known and highly respected Llangollen resident, commissioner of income tax, and the first treasurer of Bala's Methodist College); William Morgan (a Llangollen brewer); Charles Richards (the founder of the Llangollen-based firm of solicitors and bankers, Charles Richards and Sons); Rev. Dr John Pritchard (a Baptist minister in Llangollen); and James Clarke (schoolmaster at the Llangollen British School).

Discussions at the meeting initially went rather smoothly, with recommendations being made that route chosen should be the one that brought the greatest benefit to the town and that is should join the main Shrewsbury to Chester line at the nearest possible point, making the line as short as possible.

However, a jolt in the proverbial tracks came when the discussions began about where exactly the new line would leave the Shrewsbury to Chester line and which side of the River Dee it would follow. The vested interests of the various individuals present were about to rise to the surface, as many stood to make considerable financial gain depending on the route chosen.

It was to be the distinguished Henry Robertson that started the debate, regretting that the disagreement regarding the route the line should take was delaying its construction. Back in 1846, Robertson had suggested a route leaving the Shrewsbury to Chester line at Cefn, about 1 mile south of Ruabon, before passing Plas Kynaston, crossing the canal near Trevor Hall and terminating in Llangollen in a field above the canal.

By the time of the meeting, Robertson had changed his mind about the approach and terminus in Llangollen. Crossing the land in front of Trevor Hall would be an expensive proposition and to account for this, Robertson suggested that the railway should cross the canal nearer to Sun Bank, then running adjacent to the turnpike road (the present day A539), before terminating in a field between the Llangollen Vicarage and a woollen mill. Part of the vicarage land would be used for the erection of the station and Robertson was sure that the Vicar (Rev. William Edwards who was in attendance at the meeting) would show no opposition to this. He was quickly interrupted by Edwards, who reminded him that this was a matter for the Bishop and not for him as vicar of the parish.

There were a number of vocal and high-profile opponents to Robertson's proposed route along the northern side of the Dee. The meeting's chairman Colonel R. Middleton Biddulph, along with T. E. Dickin and G. H. Whalley all had an interest in seeing a route adopted from the Llangollen Road station, running to Llangollen along the southern side of the Dee via Froncysyllte. Biddulph and Dickin both owned property along the southern route, while Whalley voiced his concerns that there would be a steep gradient and sharp bend at the point where Robertson was proposing to join the main line at Cefn. Whalley added that it was also not advisable to erect a junction so near to the large embankment and Cefn Viaduct there.

In principle at least, a route along the south side of the Dee did have its merits. It would be a much shorter route and, therefore, much cheaper to construct than Robertson's route to the north. However, it was to be just one short statement from Robertson that would provide a crucial and crippling blow to this southern scheme: 'you would get no mineral traffic and the route would not touch one ounce of coal'.

By contrast, the northern route would tap into the iron works at Plas Kynaston, the New British Iron Company and then-active coal mines at Trefynant and Acrefair, as well as serving a much larger population. Robertson had already surveyed the area immediately around Llangollen in search of suitable sites for the new railway terminus and had failed to find one to the south of the Dee. Thinking ahead to further possible expansion, locating a station to the north of the river in Llangollen would enable a future extension westwards up the Dee Valley, should this ever be required.

One of the big questions on the minds of many at the meeting was how much the new railway would cost. Robertson had calculated that his northern route would cost approximately £40,000. About £25,000 of this would cover the purchase of the necessary land and the construction of the line, while the erection of stations would be about £15,000.

Robertson was willing to provide £5,000 from his own pocket and he announced that friends of his were willing to advance another £5,000. He was also of the opinion that he could persuade his old friend and ally Thomas Brassey to invest £10,000, so already half of the necessary funds appeared to be in hand.

While not all of the opinions and lines of argument made at the meeting were recorded or have survived orally, the points raised by one influential, and up until now somewhat reserved, gentleman present are known. Robert Piercy, the chief engineer of the New British Iron Company in Acrefair, was not in a position to offer his advice on the scheme, apparently having not been given sufficient notice of the meeting and had not had the time to study Robertson's plans. Piercy's first opinion without any detailed study was that the northern route (serving his company's premises *en route*) was the more favourable one. He was doubtful that Robertson's proposed junction with the main line near Cefn was feasible and instead suggested that it should be sited closer towards Ruabon near Rhosymedre.

As for the proposed terminus in Llangollen, Piercy suggested that this should be above the canal wharf in the town. He opined that if the hill leading from Llangollen Bridge to the Canal Wharf Bridge was rather steep, it would be very easy to construct a road to go under the canal rather than over it. For modern-day visitors to Llangollen, this suggested road would have been started immediately at the northern end of the historic Bishop Trevor's Bridge, which spans the River Dee in the centre of the town, before ploughing uphill, straight through the present Bridge End Hotel and burrowing under the canal. When compared with the massive structural and geographical changes that the new railway was destined to bring to both the bridge and the northern river bank during the early 1860s, the route of Piercy's proposed access road would have caused relatively little upheaval.

It was soon becoming apparent that there was still a major difference of opinion among the engineering experts present at the meeting. Whalley and Dickin, who both supported a southern route, proposed that the meeting should be deferred until Robertson's plan had been fully examined in every detail.

Robertson was determined that there should be no more deferments and that enough time had already been lost since 1846 because of deferment after deferment. Indeed, many of the locals at the meeting were getting greatly worried about the trend of the discussions and were afraid that no definite plan would be accepted. To settle the matter once and for all, one of the most highly respected Llangollen residents in the room, Ebenezer Cooper, decided to get the ball rolling. With support from a Mr Low, Cooper proposed the following resolution which was greeted with a loud round of applause (from *Llangollen Station: A History* by Paul Lawton):

> That this meeting will support a line of railway from a point near Cefn Station on the Shrewsbury Chester line, passing on the north side of the river and terminating as near the town of Llangollen as engineering reasons will permit.

Apart from locating the new line to the north of the River Dee, the resolution was vague and broad enough to keep the majority of the individuals present happy. The details would be decided by a dedicated committee at a later date. What mattered to most was that Llangollen was now about to get its very own railway—an umbilical cord into the rest of the developing nationwide network. For those fearing that the project would be stillborn, concrete evidence of the determination and commitment to the new line came in the pages of the local newspaper just nearly three weeks later.

On 13 November, a public notice appeared within the *Wrexham Advertiser* that an application was being made to Parliament:

> For an act to incorporate a Company to construct and maintain a railway commencing near the 3rd Bridge from Cefn Station over the Shrewsbury and Chester Line and terminating in a field near Llangollen Vicarage.

As was customary at the time, a public notice also had to be placed in London newspaper, with the *London Gazette* of 26 November making the announcement. As well as the construction of the line, power was also sought to 'extend a certain tramway leading from an inclined plane, from the Trevor Lime Rocks' to connect into it near Sun Bank. An intensive period of limestone quarrying and lime production was already occurring along parts of the Dee Valley's northern side, particularly in the area around Sun Bank and Trevor and the railway company was keen to tap into this.

However, at the same time, another company was also canvassing for local support. The construction of a railway from Ruabon to Denbigh via Llangollen was being proposed and a public meeting was summoned in support of the scheme, as a means of connecting the Vale of Clwyd with East Denbighshire and the industrial Midlands. The proposed scheme ultimately came to nothing, but the

Wrexham Advertiser described the first portion of the intended route in its edition of 27 November:

> Leaving Ruabon 1,700 yards to the southwest of the present station, then through the gardens of Plas Madoc, above Sun Bank, Llandyn, the Wern, the site of the Llangollen Grammar School, and terminating with a station near Maes yr Ychen in the neighbourhood of Valle Crucis Abbey in the parish of Llantysilio.

The Vale of Llangollen Railway

Robertson was keen to progress his proposed railway plan onwards in order to quash any delays from other competing schemes. By 4 December, 'The Vale of Llangollen Railway Co.' had been officially formed with a capital of £45,000, available to investors in 4,500 shares of £5. Robertson was appointed chief engineer and the cost of construction had been increased slightly to £9,000 per mile.

For a relatively short stretch of railway, there were a considerable number of earthworks that needed to be built. A deep cutting was needed to get the railway through the Cefn sandstone in and around Acrefair, which would prove to be a useful supply of sandstone for structures along the line. A further series of cuttings and embankments were required along the 5-mile length, the most noticeable being the long embankment in the central section between Bryn Howel and Sun Bank. The railway was built as a single track, with space for doubling if the traffic levels ever warranted it. Bridges carrying roads or footpaths over the railway were built to allow a second track to pass underneath then if required, whereas the majority of underbridges were built for a single track only and would then need to be widened at a later date.

While most of the line was to be built through mainly agricultural and relatively undeveloped areas, the Railway Company nonetheless had to purchase the necessary parcels of land piecemeal from the various landowners along the route. Following Robertson's original plans, the railway purchased the vicarage on the outskirts of Llangollen; a building which went on to become the Woodlands Hotel before being demolished to make way for the present-day Llangollen Health Centre. The Vicarage had been built by Rev. Robert Wynne-Eyton in 1816 and was purchased by the railway in 1858 along with just over 4 acres of land for the princely sum of £4,000.

The money raised from the sale enabled a new vicarage to be built on the south side of Llangollen. Following the death of Rev. William Edwards on 21 June 1868, Rev. Enoch Rhys James moved into the new vicarage a month later and remained there until 1895. He complained that the location of the new vicarage meant that in wet weather, water from the hill above his house would enter his well water. Crucially (at least for him), on its way downslope, this water would pass through Fron Bache graveyard and be contaminated by the non-conformist bodies buried there.

On 1 August 1859, the Vale of Llangollen Railway Act received its Royal Assent, meaning that work could start on building the new line. Interestingly, the Act laid out the maximum rates that passengers could be charged for travel in the three different classes of carriage. Passengers conveyed in a first-class carriage could not be charged more than three pence per mile, with limits of two pence per mile for second class and one penny farthing per mile for third class.

A ceremonial cutting of the first sod took place on 1 September, with the honour falling to the wife of Colonel Tottenham, the chairman of the new Railway Company.

The railway's contractors, Brassey and Field, promised that the line to Llangollen would be completed by 1 May 1861, but even at an early stage in the construction, it was becoming the general consensus locally that this target date would not be met. Progress on the extensive series of earthworks, required to provide a relatively level trackbed for the new line through the undulating terrain of the Dee Valley, was slow. As reported in the *Llangollen Advertiser* in November 1860, 'a great number' of navvies and masons were working in gangs along the route.

However, even the weather appeared to be conspiring against the new railway. December 1860 was uncommonly wet and slowed the progress right down. The following January saw work again at a standstill because of severe frost and heavy snow.

Yet, for all the physical challenges being faced, the greatest obstacle to completing the railway early was finance. As can be imagined, the railway scheme caused a great deal of excitement in the local area. However, this did not materialise itself into a particularly steady flow of capital from the townsfolk of Llangollen. The *Llangollen Advertiser* challenged the contractors on whether they would be still able to complete the work by 1 May 1861 as originally proposed. Brassey and Field replied that they were men of their word and were aiming to meet their own deadline if the money was forthcoming.

In a time where religion was still a fundamental part of daily life, the *Llangollen Advertiser* was sorry to see so many men working on the line on Sundays, 'for our part rather than that the Lord's Day be profaned, let the opening of the line be delayed a few weeks'.

Construction continued and during December, a goods train became the first to arrive into Llangollen. The necessary infrastructure and facilities were still not in place to facilitate the introduction of a passenger service, so it was to be well into the following year before permission was granted to start transporting people. On 2 June 1862, hundreds of people congregated at the railway's Vicarage Terminus in Llangollen to witness the inauguration of the passenger service.

The Great Western Railway (GWR) operated the line from the outset for 60 per cent of the returns; this arrangement was due to the Vale of Llangollen Railway Company not having any locomotives or rolling stock of its own.

2

Onwards to Corwen and Bala

Even from the outset, Llangollen was never seen to be the permanent terminus for the new railway service and thoughts quickly turned to continuing the line westwards along the Dee Valley. The GWR operated the Vale of Llangollen Railway from the outset and saw the line as the first step in its attempt to gain access to the west coast of Wales.

The town of Corwen lay around 10 miles to the west of Llangollen and was already a well-established and locally important settlement in its own right. While it had not benefitted from the canal link enjoyed by Llangollen, Corwen had long been a stopping place for travellers and had become known as the 'Crossroads of North Wales'. It does perhaps seem a little unfair for Pigot's Trade Directory of 1835 to describe Corwen as 'an inconsiderate market-town in the parish of its name'.

The Llangollen and Corwen Railway

In November 1859, barely five weeks after the Vale of Llangollen Railway's public meeting, the formation of a Llangollen and Corwen Railway was announced in the *London Gazette* newspaper. The proposal received Royal Assent on 6 August 1860, with The Llangollen and Corwen Railway Act giving the new company the power to construct:

> A railway commencing by a junction with the Vale of Llangollen Railway, as authorized by 'The Vale of Llangollen Railway Act, 1859' at the Llangollen terminus thereof in the Parish of Llangollen and County of Denbigh, and terminating in a Garden occupied by James Walch with the Glyndwr Arms Hotel in the Parish of Corwen and County of Merioneth.

The towns of Llangollen and Corwen were (and, of course, still are) connected by the meandering valley of the River Dee, which passes through a narrow gorge about 1 mile west of Llangollen before gradually widening out upstream towards Corwen. The only major settlements at the time were the villages of Glyndyfrdwy and Carrog.

The chairman of the new railway was again Colonel Tottenham, with Henry Robertson being appointed as its chief engineer. The pair had already been busy acquiring land along the proposed route and this was soon to prove invaluable for the advancement of the railway westwards.

In the first edition of the *Llangollen Advertiser* on 2 November 1860, there is an account of the Llangollen and Corwen Railway Company's first half-yearly meeting at the Town Hall there. The company's secretary proudly reported on the successful application to Parliament over the previous summer and that the new railway had the general support of the local landowners through which it would pass.

In the same vein as the Vale of Llangollen Railway, the new railway to Corwen would be initially constructed as a single line, with earthworks being designed to accommodate future doubling wherever possible. The exceptions to this would be within the gorge around the Chain Bridge and Llantysilio, where the required viaduct over the Eirianallt stream would be constructed to accommodate just a single track, along with the 689-yard Rhysgog (Berwyn) Tunnel about half a mile further west.

It was agreed that the cost of the surveys and of obtaining the Act of Incorporation would not exceed £2,500. Those present at the meeting were informed that as soon as all the necessary arrangements for acquiring the land had been made and the new route precisely set out, works would commence on cutting the new tunnel. Being the line's biggest engineering feature, its excavation would govern the completion of the entire line.

Nine directors were elected for the new company, with many also having held positions on the Vale of Llangollen Railway's committee that had been set up two years previously. Among them were W. H. Darby (the manager of Brymbo steelworks), Alexander Reid (a young Scotsman who had been persuaded by Robertson to join him at Brymbo in the early 1840s and now resided in Llantysilio), and Ebeneser Cooper (who had been so influential in getting the ball rolling on the Vale of Llangollen Railway two years previously). The Llangollen solicitor, Charles Richards, was appointed secretary with an annual salary of £100, while a Mr Patchett of Shrewsbury and Mr Edwards of Corwen would earn an annual salary of £10 each as the company's auditors.

The cutting of the first sod took place at the new Berwyn Tunnel on 1 March 1862 and shortly afterwards, there were reports in the local press that four men with a wheelbarrow had been seen working around the tunnel site. The tunnel burrowed its way deep under a hairpin bend on Telford's important Holyhead Road (the modern day A5), although the traveller on neither transport artery would have noticed the presence of the other in this remote location. It is estimated that the tunnel shortened the route of the railway by some 3 miles and removed the need for some sharp curves had the true course of the River Dee been followed.

By the end of the following June, the 'tunnellers' had gone on strike demanding more pay and were replaced by around 100 navvies. Work continued at either end of the single-bore tunnel, with the aim of meeting in the middle. For reasons that are still unknown, work on the Corwen side came to a standstill in September 1863 but soon resumed. By October 1864, 'only 30 yards of the Berwyn Tunnel remained to be completed' and the following month a hole had been made through the middle of the tunnel large enough for a man to crawl through. The hole was eventually widened out to complete the tunnel and when the two sections were connected up there was only a slight difference in their alignments.

The tunnel bore was cut through the Elwy Formation of silty mudstones, which date back to the Silurian period some 420–440 million years ago. The nature of the rock here meant that the tunnel walls were strong and stable enough to be left unlined, although a brick cladding would later be added by the GWR.

While work on the tunnel was being prepared, some serious issues had arisen in Llangollen that could have completely derailed the entire project. The Vale of Llangollen's original Vicarage terminus was located on the eastern fringes of the town and to extend the line westwards would mean removing the many obstacles that had been built over the years along the northern banks of the River Dee.

Opposite the present Bridge End Hotel, then known as the Pen y Bont Inn, was the old public water pump known as 'Pistill Penybont'. This old hand pump provided drinking water for many and now lay directly in the way of the new railway. Worse still, the townsfolk had an ancient right to take washing water from the Dee and the line was projected to cut straight through the steps that gave access to the river.

Protracted negotiations with the Llangollen Board of Health were finally concluded with the Railway Company being able to purchase this important parcel of riverside land, on the proviso that the old pump would be replaced by two new ones nearby: one for drinking water and one for washing water.

Yet, there were even more obstacles to overcome before the railway could pass completely through the northern part of the town. In its path stood the four-arch bridge over the River Dee, connecting both parts of the town. This stone structure was considered to be one of the 'Wonders of Wales' and had been standing since at least 1346. At its northern end, the Old Toll Gate House also stood proudly recounting a time when tolls needed to be paid in order to travel along certain roads in the area.

The simplest option would have been to add another arch to the northern end of the bridge, but the road deck was not high enough to give the required clearance for trains to safely pass under it. Lowering the level of the trackbed would have taken the railway closer to the river level, making it more liable to flooding. Instead, work commenced on reprofiling the entire deck of the bridge, sloping the road deck upwards to give the required headroom for passing trains.

Yet, crossing under the historic bridge was not the end of the challenges faced by the Railway Company. Between the present-day Abbey Road and the river bank were some sixty cottages that were mostly the homes of Llangollen weavers. These buildings were located around the Llangollen Green and would have been a substantial obstacle for the railway builders had it not been for the foresight of Henry Robertson. As it transpired, Robertson had bought the properties sometime before, with the intention that his tenants could then be moved when the land was needed for the new line. The tenants were housed in temporary accommodation until their new houses in Princess Street on the southern side of the river were ready for occupation.

The old Llangollen Green, though, was potentially more of an obstacle since its free use by the townsfolk was protected by an Act of Parliament. Back in 1839, the Middelton Biddulph family of Chirk Castle had gained legal protection for the two acres of land to be reserved and safeguarded as grounds for recreation. In 1857, the newly formed Llangollen Board of Health had directed a letter to the General Board of Health in London asking for the authority to fence, improve, and maintain the Green and this was duly granted.

Evidently, the politics of the Llangollen Board of Health changed over the ensuing few years as by 1861, Robertson had managed to persuade them to sell the Green to the Llangollen and Corwen Railway Company for £150.

Taken from the Bishop Trevor bridge at the eastern end of the station, this fascinating Victorian view of Llangollen dates from between 1894 and 1897. By May 1898, work had commenced on the new footbridge and excursion platforms, transforming the station to handle the growing footfall of passengers. The locomotive appears to be to an Armstrong 517 Class 0-4-2T design.

The sale of the Green caused a lot of local opposition and criticism, with some questioning of whether the Board had the legal right to sell in the first place. Lengthy and at times somewhat tedious negotiations rumbled on for the next ten years until the situation was fully resolved. The L&CR agreed to secure and hand over a suitable piece of land to the town for use as a new Recreation Ground, while the Board of Health handed back the £150 in return.

Yet, with all the obstacles faced by the railway builders in Llangollen now overcome, construction work was able to continue unabated during the early 1860s. The path of the railway had cut a swathe through the northern bank of the town, requiring the demolition and rehousing of many locals, major modifications to a 500-year-old river bridge and the establishment of a new public green and water pumps. The influence of Robertson and the L&CR had grown significantly since the establishment of its predecessor, the Vale of Llangollen Railway, only a few years before.

Architecturally, the buildings along the L&CR were designed to complement the landscape as well as making a statement of importance and permanence. The L&CR turned to a Shropshire based architect for the design of its station buildings to serve Llangollen, Berwyn, Glyndyfrdwy, Llansantffraid Glyndyfrdwy (destined to be named Carrog when it opened) and Corwen. Samuel Pountney Smith had been born in Munslow, near to Craven Arms, in 1812 and had learnt the trades of builder and architect within his uncle in the Severn Valley near Bridgnorth.

Smith's work had been strongly influenced by A. W. N. Pugin and his designs were mainly in the Early English Gothic style. The majority of his output was mainly in relation to churches, designing new ones and carrying out alterations or restorations to others, which included the remodelling and enlargement of St Collen's Church in Llangollen between 1864 and 1867.

Smith's designs for the new L&CR stations were intended to replicate the lodges on a great estate. At the time, the resulting buildings were described as 'all of a very chaste and appropriate character, and very far superior in architectural design to that of railway stations generally'. At the three intermediate stations, the station master's house was attached to the operational part of the building, with those at Glyndyfrdwy and Carrog being nearly identical in appearance. Due to the restricted space available, a third floor was added to the Berwyn station master's house to compensate for its smaller footprint.

In Corwen, trains had already been terminating in the town as early as October 1864, but these were on the metals of the Denbigh, Ruthin and Corwen Railway from the north. Discussions between the DR&CR and the L&CR seem to have been very amicable, with an agreement being reached for a new joint station in the town once the line from Llangollen had been completed. The single tracks of the DR&CR and the L&CR met near Green Lane to the east of the town centre and approached the new station in parallel. This gave the impression of double track, whereas in reality each was operated independently.

By 1865, the L&CR had been progressed enough to enable Charles Tottenham to run a private train between the two towns on 14 January for the benefit of his invited guests. A month later, the first goods train ran on the line and in a truly charitable gesture, it consisted of seven wagons of best Broughton coal for the poor of nearby Llandrillo and Llandderfel, personally gifted by Henry Robertson.

On Monday 13 March, a private train consisting of two carriages and a goods van conveyed a gentleman who had been staying in Llangollen's Hand Hotel, to Corwen. The train stopped just before the Berwyn Tunnel to pick up Colonel Tottenham and his family. Tottenham continued on by road to Bala, while the rest of the family returned having enjoyed their trip. The *Wrexham Weekly Advertiser* recorded on 18 March that 'several trains of coal have been taken to Corwen and it is obvious from the small number of carts seen passing up and down the Corwen road that the inhabitants avail themselves of it'.

The following month, the *Advertiser* recorded that about 77 railway carriages worth of passengers had arrived at Llangollen station on Good Friday alone. It would appear that the drizzly weather on the day did little to dampen spirits.

An important milestone was reached on 24 April when the L&CR was visited by the Government's railway inspector Captain Rich. A special inspection train comprising two locomotives and a carriage was prepared and he spent six hours travelling the length of the line. He was accompanied by a small party of gentlemen, including Brassey and Field (the line's contractors) and Colonel Tottenham. The inspector recommended a few minor alterations but on the whole approved of the line.

The opening of the new line linking Llangollen and Corwen caused a real stir among the locals and celebration in the air. The *Carnarvon and Denbigh Herald* reported on the event in great detail in their edition on 29 April 1865 and noted:

> Soon … we arrived at Corwen, where large numbers of persons were assembled, who welcomed heartily the arrival of the preliminary opening train. The line we should state is eleven miles long, and will be opened probably early in the ensuing month, as it is only waiting for the satisfaction of the government inspector to be opened for traffic. The engineer was that indefatigable pioneer of railways, Henry Robertson Esq., M.P., and Messrs Brassey and Field, the contractors.

The local media were quick to point out the new travel opportunities that the railway offered, stating that the townsfolk of Corwen could now reach London by rail in six hours and forty-five minutes. Liverpool was just two hours and forty-five minutes away, while a journey to Manchester was achievable in three hours. Today, with the closure of the line as a through route, the journey time to Liverpool by public transport is only a little better than that in 1865; taking around two hours to Liverpool and two hours and forty-five minutes to Manchester. However, all the controversy of closing the line was just under a century away as locals and visitors alike celebrated and adapted to their new railway.

Not everyone was impressed with the new Llangollen and Corwen Railway, as is demonstrated in the *Wrexham Weekly Advertiser*'s May 1865 report on the line's opening:

One cannot help being struck by the pleasing and agreeable contrast between the clear, comfortable and spacious carriages of the Vale of Clwyd line (which reached Corwen via Denbigh and Ruthin) and the dull, dingy and uncomfortable wagons of the Great Western.

Even before all the celebrations had completely subsided, there were signs that there was an underlying problem with the route parts of the new line had taken. In August 1865, torrential rain caused serious damage to the western section of the line requiring immediate attention. Around Glyndyfrdwy, several yards of embankment were washed away, leaving the sleepers exposed, while near Carrog a culvert was partially swept away. Repairs were soon affected and service was resumed within just a few days.

In a bid to keep down construction costs, the route of the line between Glyndyfrdwy and Corwen had been designed to take advantage of the wide and level valley floor. This meant that in some locations, the trackbed was only gently raised above the floodplain, making it potentially susceptible to damage during periods of prolonged or excessive rainfall. The section immediately around Bonwm, about 1 mile east of Corwen, was particularly susceptible to flooding and erosion of the trackbed. Throughout the line's history, contingency plans were constantly under review and the District Civil Engineer kept a watchful eye on the local river levels.

The Corwen and Bala Railway

In October 1860, public meetings were held in Bala and in the Owain Glyndwr Hotel in Corwen. The main objective was to discuss the proposed railway schemes then being prepared in the area. Work was already in hand on the Denbigh, Ruthin and Corwen Railway that was to terminate in Corwen from the north, while the combination of the Vale of Llangollen and Llangollen and Corwen Railways would link in from the east.

Colonel Tottenham, the chairman of the Llangollen and Corwen Railway, attended the meeting in Corwen and was keen to stress that care should be taken when planning the route of the line to Bala. He had been in discussion with several wealthy quarry owners who had expressed an interest in a branch line from Bala to Ffestiniog. Tottenham believed that a large amount of slate traffic would be generated by this extension and that plans for the Corwen to Bala route should be designed to incorporate this.

When pressed on which railway company should take on the construction of the Corwen to Bala line, Tottenham responded that it should be the one 'in the best position to do so' and the other company should assist wherever possible.

Meanwhile at the opposite end of the proposed line 'the most stormy meeting that ever took place in Bala' was being held in the town hall. The room was packed and the topic certainly stirred up much emotion among those in attendance: 'the various speakers were frequently interrupted in their addresses by hisses and shoutings of the noisiest description'.

The purpose of the meeting was to discuss the proposal for a West Midland, Shrewsbury and Coast of Wales railway that was then being mooted. The meeting itself nearly fell at the first hurdle, when a Mr Jones of Bryn Tegid was voted to chair the meeting but initially declined to take the seat. After being repeatedly urged to do so, Jones opened the proceedings and called upon the proposed line's engineer take to the stage.

Representing a West Midland Line scheme at the meeting was its engineer, Mr Wilson. The scheme envisaged building a line from Shrewsbury up the Tanat Valley to Llangynog, after which it would tunnel through the Berwyn Mountains before emerging near Llandrillo. The tunnel itself would have been 1.5 miles in length—a massive undertaking in its own right. The line would then continue on to Bala, Blaenau Ffestiniog, Porthmadog, and ultimately Porthdinllaen on the North Wales coast.

Over the course of the meeting, it was established that the scheme of 90 miles would cost around £900,000, which was based on the standard estimate of £10,000 per mile of track. The main driving force behind the scheme appears to have been the supposed 'urgent demand' of West Midlands-based manufacturers to gain access to the sea. Supporters wanted to see free access by the same train from London and Oxford to Shrewsbury, Corwen, Bala, and beyond.

The proposal and plans for the West Midlands scheme were deposited in the Board of Trade's offices in London on 30 November 1860. The scheme came fairly early in Parliament, although a branch line up the Tanat Valley to Llangynog would later come to fruition over four decades later in 1904.

Discussions rumbled on into 1862, when two competing schemes emerged. The first was Thomas Savin's Corwen, Bala and Barmouth Railway which would have been a continuation of his Denbigh, Ruthin and Corwen Railway already under construction. In April, the scheme began to unravel in front of Parliamentary committee, when it was revealed that if Savin got control of the Barmouth to Corwen route he would control a vast area of North Wales. There was a high risk that Savin would route traffic the 'long way round' via Rhyl rather than relinquish it to his competitor, the Great Western Railway.

The other scheme had originally been called the Corwen, Bala and Porthmadog Railway, but by the time it was being examined by the Parliamentary committee, it had been reduced to just a Corwen to Bala line and renamed accordingly. The scheme had the backing of the GWR and gained Parliamentary approval.

The Corwen and Bala Railway Company received its Royal Assent on 30 June 1862. At the same time, another GWR-backed scheme—the Bala and Dolgelly Railway—gained its approval. The GWR's plans to reach the Cambrian Coast seemed to be coming to fruition and just over ten miles would remain beyond Dolgelly before its dream would be finally realised. Rejoicing in Paddington was destined to be short-lived, but that is a tale best saved for Volume 2.

With official approval to commence works, the Corwen and Bala Railway Company set out raising the required capital to build its new line. The route of the railway would be just under 11 miles (10 miles 72 chains) in length and would have intermediate stations for the villages of Cynwyd, Llandrillo, and Llandderfel. By following the wide Dee valley for most of its length, the new line would be the easiest section of the rapidly expanding cross-country Ruabon to Dolgelly route to be built. The only major engineering features were two girder bridges across the River Dee and a 157-yard tunnel at Llandderfel.

The capital needed for this was £160,000 which was considerably higher per mile than the standard estimate being banded around two years previously. Keen to show its support, the GWR contributed £40,000, while the Vale of Llangollen Railway and Llangollen and Corwen Railway companies each contributed £10,000. Shareholders and investors provided the remainder of the capital.

Construction worked soon commenced in earnest and on 16 July 1866, the first section from Corwen to Llandrillo opened to the public. The remaining section contained the two river crossings and the tunnel, but this was completed without major incident on 1 April 1868.

3

Ruabon to Llangollen

Ruabon (0 miles 0 chains)

Situation
The town of Ruabon marked the start of what was commonly known as the 'Barmouth Road' among locomotive crews. For prospective passengers, the journey across the width of Wales would involve encompass lakes, rivers and moorland, before skirting along the edge of an estuary and jubilantly crossing it on an impressive trestle bridge on the final approach to Barmouth.

For such a scenic and breathtaking journey, it is fair to say that Ruabon offered few hints of what was to come. The town remained largely industrial in nature, being well-endowed with large deposits of iron, coal, and clay. In the 1850s, the English writer George Borrow described Ruabon in *Wild Wales* (1862):

> A large village about half way between Wrexham and Llangollen. I observed in this place nothing remarkable, but an ancient church. My way from hence lay nearly west. I ascended a hill, from the top of which I looked down into a smoky valley. I descended, passing by a great many collieries, in which I observed grimy men working amidst smoke and flame.

With the arrival of the railway in 1846, Ruabon temporarily became a terminus of a line from Chester and Wrexham. The station was built to the west of the town, with the site spanning the River Eitha. The station's buildings were designed by the architect Thomas Penson in an Italianate design and opened on 4 November 1846. Just two years later, the role of the station changed entirely, with the opening of the new line southwards to Shrewsbury. Ruabon went being from a bustling terminus to a quieter intermediate station almost overnight and was not really even considered to be a railhead for the Llangollen and the Dee Valley; this role fell to nearby Llangollen Road station to the south.

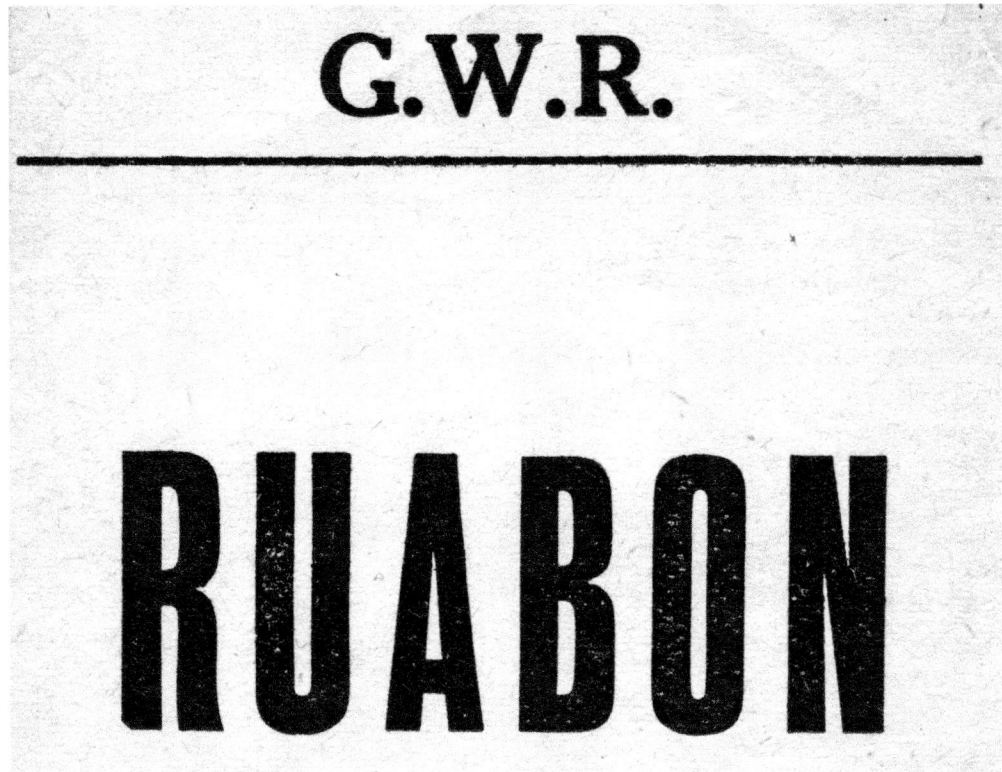

Above: Ruabon GWR luggage label.

Below: Ivatt-designed 2MT 2-6-0 No. 46508 approaches Ruabon station from the north with a three-coach passenger service bound towards Barmouth. Note the Ruabon North signal box in the background, which had opened in 1918 and controlled the line to Ponkey.

The overbridge carrying the B5097 road up to Wynne Hall at the northern end of the station gives a superb vantage point of 46508 slowing for its call at Ruabon. The building in the centre background formerly housed the old refreshment rooms.

No. 1019 *County of Merioneth* at Ruabon, June 1962.

Facilities

In 1860, the station buildings were replaced at the suggestion of Henry Robertson, ahead of the Vale of Llangollen Railway's opening. The new building was designed in a neo-Tudor style that was destined to become that adopted for the stations on the Llangollen to Corwen Railway.

Passengers approaching the station would have been faced by two sets of doors. The pair on the left gave access to the parcels office and cloakroom, while the pair on the right led into the station's booking hall. Surprisingly there was no fireplace provided within this room, although the associated Booking Office for the staff did feature a small corner grate.

Proceeding out onto the platform, a substantial glazed canopy extending to the platform edge provided protection from the elements. Separate doorways off the platform gave access to the station master's office, inspector's office, general first class waiting room, and separate ladies' first and third class waiting rooms. Passengers who had a long wait or journey ahead of them could sample the publications available from the Wymans' Bookstall.

The platform arrangement consisted of two platforms for the Chester to Shrewsbury line, then a bay platform on the western side of the station from which many Llangollen line trains started. A covered footbridge linked these platforms, with a continuation on the Down side leading to the original refreshments rooms. By the end of the nineteenth century, the Down platform had been reconstructed and widened. A run round loop was provided within the bay platform to improve the operational flexibility and this proved particularly useful for services terminating at Ruabon off the Barmouth line. A new building was provided on this incorporating a new Refreshment Room, General Waiting Room and lavatories. These could not have been built soon enough as pressure had already been mounting for improved facilities at the station.

During the first few years of the Ruabon's role as a junction, passenger provision was sparse and the connections between the two lines were poor. The subject quickly became a source of many complaints from the locals. In February 1864, one irate passenger wrote to the *Wrexham Advertiser*:

> If I leave Wrexham at 12.25 I must wait at Ruabon an hour and twenty minutes for a train to Llangollen. Or if I leave Llangollen at 12.05, I must walk up and down the platform at Ruabon for an hour and fifteen minutes for a train to Wrexham. Again, if I leave Wrexham at 8.47 p.m. or Llangollen at 8.30, forty minutes have to be passed in a cold, cheerless booking office. Now if this arrangement cannot be altered, why not provide a good 'refreshment room' when passengers, compelled to wait may do so without running the risk of taking cold, and where they would be able to enjoy themselves during the time the company [GWR] compel them to remain?

It is believed that during the 1880s, the GWR produced proposals to construct a large workshop complex at Ruabon in which they could build and maintain their steam locomotives. The plan was seemingly abandoned when terms could not

Ivatt-designed 2MT 2-6-0 46509, carrying a 6C (Croes Newydd) shed code plate, enters Ruabon station *c.* 1963. The station appears to be well kept, with the buffer stops of the bay platform being visible in the background.

No. 4472 *Flying Scotsman* at Ruabon, April 1963.

No. 1011 *County of Chester* at Ruabon, September 1964.

Blowing off impatiently at the head of a Birkenhead-bound train, ex-LMS Black Five 4-6-0 No. 45353 awaits departure from Ruabon, *c.* 1963.

LMS-built Jubilee 6P 4-6-0 No. 45699 *Galatea* makes an imposing sight at the head of a Down passenger service *c*. 1963. A series of parcels are being loaded onto the train from a standard GWR four-wheeled trolley for onwards dispatch across the country.

A three-coach service off the Llangollen line, headed by now preserved BR Standard 4-6-0 No. 75029, awaits departure from Ruabon. The locomotive was by now allocated to Croes Newydd shed, having been transferred there during week commencing 9 March 1963.

No. 4472 *Flying Scotsman* at Ruabon, April 1963.

Rail tours and enthusiasts' specials commonly feature in views from the early 1960s and this is no exception. BR-built Manor 4-6-0 No. 7827 *Lydham Manor* prepares to depart from Ruabon with the Talyllyn Railway Preservation Society's AGM Special on 26 September 1964. Already preserved GWR Small Prairie No. 4555 is tucked in behind the Manor. This was to be the last time a rail tour covered the Ruabon to Barmouth line in its entirety before closure.

The footplate crew prepare BR Manor 4-6-0 No. 7827 *Lydham Manor* for departure with the Talyllyn Railway Preservation Society's AGM Special on 26 September 1964.

No. 44680 at Ruabon, March 1967.

Nos 7827 *Lydham Manor* and 7819 *Hinton Manor* at Ruabon Middle Box, April 1963.

On 25 April 1964, No. 4079 Pendennis Castle heads south from the station light engine having worked a Ffestiniog Railway Special railtour and is seen passing beneath the Ruabon to Llangollen road bridge (now the A539).

be agreed with Sir Watkin Williams Wynn on whose land the works were to be built. In 1905, the station refreshment rooms were purchased by the GWR from Sir Watkin William Wynn, with James Cresswell Murless of the nearby Wynnstay Arms remaining as their tenant.

Life at Ruabon

In 1893, the station master at Ruabon was a Mr G. E. Fussell who had previously held the same position at Llangollen. Very soon into his new position, Fussell became aware of numerous instances of goods items being stolen or going missing from the adjoining goods yard. Further investigations led to the arrest of three railway employees (a foreman, pointsman, and shunter) in late March for pilfering goods. After this, the unofficial practice seems to have ceased.

There are a number of instances were temptation got the better of railway employees. However, not every item that went missing from Ruabon station was taken with the intent of self-improvement and financial gain. In June 1873, intoxication was very much the intent for two men when a barrel of rum arrived by train. One evening a James Carless was seen removing the tarpaulin from over the barrel, while his accomplice David Bowen climbed inside the railway wagon and abstracted about 1.5 pints of rum (valued at four shillings). Both men then headed towards a nearby pointsman's hut where they apparently enjoyed their plunder. Bowen was acquitted of the charge, but Carless was sentenced to six months imprisonment with hard labour.

By then preserved GWR 4-4-0 No. 3440 *City of Truro* stands in the bay platform at Ruabon on 30 March 1957, having earlier brought in a Ffestiniog Railway Society special from Wolverhampton. Note the ornate GWR full harp lamp on the platform behind the loco's tender.

Above: An additional view of GWR 4-4-0 No. 3440 *City of Truro* at Ruabon while taking part in the Ffestiniog Railway Society special from Wolverhampton in 1957.

Right: No. 3440 at Ruabon, March 1957.

The vast majority of passengers commencing their journeys from Ruabon would have been either locals or holidaymakers during the late 1800s and early 1900s. However, following the outbreak of the First World War, there is a curious tale of two runaway German officers who used the station to make their escape. In April 1915, the pair escaped from the German internment camp near Denbigh and apparently arrived in a somewhat worn-out condition at Ruabon about 5 p.m. There they enquired about the next train for London and were informed that it would leave at 5.47 p.m. The pair were then noted boarding this train and it is believed they were hoping to reach Paddington, before escaping across the English Channel. It is unclear how long they managed to evade capture or whether they were successful in their escape bid.

Signalling

The complexity and scale of the railway system around Ruabon is highlighted in the fact that at one stage there were five signal boxes controlling the station area. Signalling improvements and remodelling enabled this to be reduced to three: Ruabon North, Ruabon Middle, and Ruabon South signal boxes.

Ruabon North box was located a short distance away from the station in the Wrexham direction and had opened on 3 November 1918. The thirty-one-lever frame-controlled access to the Ponkey branch, Down Loop, and the sidings on the north side of the station.

Ruabon Middle box was a much larger affair and contained a fifty-nine-lever frame to control the platform area, as well as the sidings on either side of the line. The box was one of the original ones from 1884 and was located overlooking the running lines and turntable to the south of the station.

Ruabon South box was located beyond the Ruabon to Llangollen road overbridge and contained a fifty-four-lever frame. The box overlooked four tracks: the two main running lines and the Up and Down Loop lines. It had opened on 2 July 1933, replacing previous smaller boxes at Llangollen Line Junction and the original Ruabon South box. The new signal box took over the control of the loop lines, sidings at Plas Madoc and, of course, the junction to Llangollen. The *Liverpool Mercury* of 20 November 1883 reports on a 'Serious Accident at Ruabon':

> Messrs. McKenzie and Holland, railway engineers, Worcester, have been fitting up a number of new signal boxes. One of these is an intermediate box, between Ruabon Station and the junction of the Llangollen and Corwen branch. While the men were engaged yesterday in fitting up the signal apparatus in this box, a stone wall at the rear, which had been built to prevent the embankment from slipping down on to the line, suddenly collapsed, and some eight tons of masonry and earth falling upon the box capsized it on to a number of waggons standing in a siding. A foreman named Thomas Nevitt of Worcester, a fitter named Richard Terry also of Worcester and Thomas Collins, a labourer living in Gobowen, were crushed beneath the fallen structure and were only extricated after considerable difficulty. They were carried to

the waiting rooms at the station, where they were examined by Dr Jones of Ruabon, who found that Collins had sustained injuries to both legs and he was taken to Wrexham Infirmary. Nevitt was badly hurt at the back of the head and on his breast and at his own request; he was taken to his lodgings in Ruabon. Terry was injured to the back and chest and he also was taken to his lodgings.

Run Down and Closure

The closure of the Llangollen line to passengers in early 1965 ended the importance of Ruabon as a railway junction and interchange station. Rails remained from Llangollen Line Junction as far as Llangollen Goods Junction until 1968, when demolition crews commenced work removing the remaining infrastructure and track.

The coal industry around Ruabon was already in decline and this compounded the reduction in traffic passing through the goods yard. In the early 1970s, the remaining sidings were taken out, leaving just the double track running line through the station.

The rationalisation process brought about the closures of the signal boxes that once controlled the bustling sidings, loop lines, goods yard, and platforms. Ruabon North box survived until September 1965, while Ruabon South box lasted until May 1969 until succumbing. Ruabon Middle box soldiered on before signalling its last train in June 1987. However, it had already come onto the radar of the Llangollen Railway volunteers and components of the lever frame were incorporated in the reconstructed Llangollen Goods Junction signal box.

The goods yard and sidings to the east of the running line have since been redeveloped and are now partially occupied by a housing estate. The denuded bay platform and turntable pit still survive, with the land to the west of the running lines south of the station becoming engulfed in vegetation.

Acrefair (1 m 40 ch)

Significant Dates
Opened to passengers: 2 June 1862
Goods facilities withdrawn: 2 November 1964
Closed to passengers: 18 January 1965
Signal box closed: 8 January 1967

Situation
Trains bound towards Llangollen headed south-west along the Shrewsbury line for about two-thirds of a mile south of Ruabon where the two routes split. Llangollen Line Junction marked the start of a long curve away from the Chester to Shrewsbury line and from here, the line ran westwards on a steep uphill grade of 1 in 75. Initially within a shallow cutting, the line climbed up on an embankment and passed near the grounds of St John's Church before crossing over a minor

road. While the church rises up above the landscape, the railway was forced into a deep cutting through the Cefn sandstone before Acrefair station could be reached.

The church itself had been consecrated on 6 July 1837 on land donated by Sir Watkin Williams Wynn. It was built largely at his own expense, using local Cefn stone and serving the parish of Rhosymedre. The overall plan from the church's architect, Edward Welch, has been described as 'sprawlingly cruciform' with low pitched roofs and corner pinnacles. Unlike the railway, St John's still survives and is now a listed building.

While the church rises up above the landscape, the railway was forced into a deep cutting through the Cefn Sandstone before the village of Acrefair could be reached. For centuries, this large outcrop had been widely used in the locality, including the construction of the Pontcysyllte Aqueduct and Cefn Viaduct, as well as the Liverpool landmarks of St George's Hall and The Walker Art Gallery. Getting the railway through it involved a cutting over 50 feet deep and was to be the first major obstacle faced by the railway's contractors. However, this work did produce a large amount of sandstone, which could be used in the construction of bridges and other infrastructure along the new line.

Despite being excavated predominantly through solid sandstone, the deep nature of the cutting did make it prone to landslips and rockfalls. One of the earliest cases of this occurred in March 1864, as reported in the Saturday 12 March edition of the *Wrexham Advertiser*:

> A quantity of loose earth was washed down, which prevented the Sunday morning train from proceeding farther than Acrefair Station. Every precaution was taken to avoid an accident or even inconvenience to the passengers. Several men were immediately put to work to clear the rubbish, so that the evening trains passed to and fro as usual.

Perhaps the most severe landslip at Acrefair occurred some forty years later. In February 1904, when a prolonged period of rainfall resulted in over twenty tons of sandstone, soil, and other debris falling down into the eastern section of the cutting. Breakdown gangs were quickly dispatched to the scene, with single line working being temporarily adopted through the cutting. However, by 8 p.m., both tracks had reopened to traffic, with all the spoil having been removed by rail. The *Wellington Journal* reported on a similar 'Sad Fatality Near Ruabon' in its Saturday 30 September 1899 edition:

> A shocking accident occurred on Thursday on the Great Western Railway near Ruabon. The guard of an early down goods train, when passing through the deep cutting between Ruabon and Acrefair, noticed the body of a man lying near the metals in the cutting. He gave information to the officials at Acrefair Station and John Evans (Cefn Mawr) and David Parry (Acrefair Station) proceeded to the spot and found the lifeless body of James Jarvis, a married collier aged 56 years, of Cefn Mawr. The deceased was conveyed home. Dr T. Owen Jones (Acrefair) examined the

The Plas Madoc road bridge provided a superb vantage point for enthusiasts just south of Ruabon. On 25 April 1964, GWR Hall class 4-6-0 No. 4933 *Himley Hall* heads northwards towards the station with a lengthy goods train from Shrewsbury.

No. 7014 *Caerhays Castle* at Llangollen Line Junction, April 1963.

No. 4933 *Himley Hall* at Llangollen Line Junction, April 1964.

Situated nearly three-quarters of a mile south of Ruabon station, Llangollen Line Junction marked the point where the routes to Shrewsbury and Barmouth split. The junction's layout can be seen to good effect, as Ivatt 2MT 2-6-0 No. 46442 heads its short train off the Barmouth line on 21 July 1964.

A panoramic view of Llangollen Line Junction on 28 September 1963. The line to Shrewsbury is on the left, while 1944-built pannier tank No. 4683 heads a lengthy freight train off the Barmouth line.

No. 4472 *Flying Scotsman* at Llangollen Line Junction.

The Down InterCity service from London Paddington to Birkenhead passes the junction hauled by BR Modified Hall type 4-6-0 No. 6994 *Baggrave Hall* on 25 April 1964.

No. 6914 *Langton Hall* at Llangollen Line Junction, September 1963.

No. 34064 *Fighter Command* at Llangollen Line Junction, September 1963.

Nos 7827 *Lydham Manor* and 7822 *Foxcote Manor* at Llangollen Line Junction, September 1963.

Ivatt 2MT 2-6-2 No. 41201 rounds the curve away from Llangollen Line Junction with a Wrexham to Barmouth train on 25 April 1964.

BR Standard Class 4 4-6-0 No. 75024 approaches the junction with a seemingly lengthy train off the Barmouth line. The headlamps on the smokebox indicate that the train is a Class 'A' working—an express passenger service.

Nos 7801 *Anthony Manor* and 7314 at Llangollen Line Junction, September 1962.

body and found that Jarvis, who had fallen a distance of at least 80 feet, had broken his neck besides sustaining terrible injuries to his head and body. An inquest will be held.

Facilities

Acrefair station was located at the end of the cutting and served the industrialised village that had developed around the Ruabon to Llangollen Turnpike Road. The name 'Acrefair' is derived from St Mary's Acre and recalls the days when an acre of land would be dedicated to the Virgin Mary and given to a church or prior for its use.

Originally, the station featured a passing loop and a platform on the southern side of the running line. Due to the cramped location, the amount of space available for sidings and goods facilities was limited and it was not possible to provide the same arrangements as nearby Trevor. Two short sidings and small goods yard were installed behind the station's platform serving local traders and merchants. A siding was installed the Llangollen end of the loop, terminating just short of the former Ruabon to Llangollen Turnpike Road. Immediately beyond the western end of the station, passengers could catch a glimpse of the Pontcysyllte mineral branch as it passed beneath the line on its way downgrade towards Trevor.

No accommodation for the station master was provided by the Vale of Llangollen Railway; it was expected that he should live locally. His role at Acrefair also encompassed the responsibility for Trevor station and he would have been required to regularly travel between the two. By 1924, seven other members of

Looking east from the Down platform, Acrefair station appears quiet as Ivatt Mogul No. 46508 waits patiently to depart. The gradient post on the Up platform shows where the summit of this section was located.

L.M.S. Standard Class 2MT 2-6-0 No. 46509 of Croes Newydd shed calls at Acrefair with an Up passenger working on 28 May 1963. By this time, the line was already under the control of the London Midland region, with one of the posters on the station building publicising the *Condor* Anglo-Scottish Overnight Express Freight service. (*Tony Cooke/Colour Rail*)

staff were employed alongside the station master at Acrefair, comprising two clerks, two signalmen, two porters, and one checker.

Improvements

The years of 1897 to 1900 saw some considerable change for Acrefair Station. In 1897, the GWR authorised the expenditure of over £50,000 to provide double track and associated station improvements between Ruabon and Llangollen Goods Junction. Official reports indicate that the most difficult part of this work was the widening of the cutting to the east of Acrefair, with large amounts of spoil and sandstone being removed by rail.

A waiting shelter was opened on Acrefair's newly constructed Up platform, to the then universal GWR design of red and blue brick with a Welsh slate roof. A new station building was constructed in a similar style on the Down platform, comprising a booking office, general waiting room, ladies waiting room and two lavatories. A separate goods office was provided behind the booking office, where clerks were based to cater for the increasing goods traffic in the area. The canopies on both buildings were without external supports on the platform; the main girders were tied back to the rear wall of the building.

In parallel with the extensive alterations to the track layout, a new signal box was ordered in 1897 and opened the following year. As this was a time when GWR signalling was provided on a lavish scale on the line, Acrefair signal box was constructed on the Down platform and was similar to those provided at Llangollen, Glyndyfrdwy, Carrog and Llandrillo. It was of the standard hip-roofed brick variety, measuring 25 feet by 15 feet and contained a twenty-seven-lever GWR double-twist locking frame.

At a Cefn Parish Council meeting in December 1899, the councillors decided to bring the poor state of the road leading to Acrefair station to the attention of the GWR. The following February, the Council reported that there had been a large number of complaints and the GWR had promised to improve the approach road. Somewhat curiously, the clerk's response was 'the Great Western Railway improvements take a long time to bring about!'

The GWR report on the line in 1924 has the station serving a population of about 7,000 within the villages of Acrefair and Cefn. This figure seems very healthy with a large catchment area within easy reach of the station. However, all is not as it seems, for the nearby village of Cefn lay adjacent to the GWR's Chester to Shrewsbury route, with stations being provided at Cefn and (from 1906) Rhosymedre Halt.

Life at Acrefair

Life at the station was generally quiet, punctuated by the odd exciting moment. In June 1882, several railwaymen raising a large crane found themselves overpowered, resulting in serious injury. Two of the men—William Williams (a blacksmith) and Alfred Thompson (a striker/blacksmith's apprentice)—were sent directly to Wrexham Infirmary, where it was found that Williams' knee had been crushed and required an immediate operation. By all accounts, Thompson seems to have come off more lightly with his own injuries.

In June 1900, two wagon loads of chemical-filled carboys were delivered to the station from Ruabon and promptly caught fire in the mid-day sun. Local reports recall 'a scene of great animation' as station staff fought to control the ensuing blaze and save the precious cargo but to no avail.

Perhaps the busiest day in the station's history came in December 1894, when a local Baptist minister returned home from his six-month lecturing and preaching tour of the United States. A crowd of around 1,000 people was waiting at the station to greet him, before the procession marched off to a nearby church accompanied by the sound of a Salvation Army band.

Given its industrial surroundings and location, the station area could sometimes become enveloped in fog. The smoke from the adjacent Monsanto works would only add to the problem, reducing visibility and making shunting movements even more difficult for railway workers. For passengers travelling towards Ruabon, extra care had to be taken when using the foot crossing at the end of the platforms as trains could appear out of the sylvan gloom with little or no warning.

In later years, the station was overshadowed by the adjacent buildings of Hughes and Lancaster's works (later Air Products). For a time, there was a gateway leading from the Up platform into the works and in 1924, it was the firm's responsibility to ensure that this gate was kept locked. Similarly, the Down platform was connected to the nearby Cefn Mawr road by means of a set of steps.

Run Down and Closure

In common with the other stations on the line, the 1960s saw contractions in an effort to make the railway pay. The first changes occurred in 1963, when the former GWR routes north of Banbury were transferred to the London Midland region of British Railways. At Acrefair, the only noticeable change came in the style and type of posters being displayed around the station. Instead of extolling the virtues of holidaying in the Cambrian and West Country coastal resorts, posters were beginning to appear publicising 'The Condor', which was the London Midland's overnight containerised freight service between London and Glasgow.

The year 1963 did see one aspect of modernisation at Acrefair, when electrical lighting was installed inside the station buildings in place of the previous gas fittings. Any prospect of further investment evaporated with the publication of *The Reshaping of British Railways* in March 1963, more commonly known as the infamous Beeching report, which earmarked the line for closure. Notices advertising the withdrawal of the passenger services were posted the following October, with objectors having until 9 December to make their case known. The original proposed closure date in January 1964 came and went. It was to be the November before goods facilities at Acrefair were withdrawn, with passenger services lingering on until January 1965.

The line through Acrefair continued to be open for freight and the occasional railtour until 1967, but only as far as Llangollen Goods Junction. The signal box at Acrefair was officially closed on 8 January 1967. The final track lifting through the station and cutting to Llangollen Line Junction was completed by May 1969, with all the station buildings being razed to the ground.

Trevor (2 m 38 ch)

Significant Dates
Opened to passengers: 2 June 1862
Goods facilities withdrawn: 1 January 1968
Closed to passengers: 18 January 1965

Situation
On leaving Acrefair, the line crossed the main Llangollen to Ruabon road on an impressive skew arch bridge, measuring 12 feet wide and 23 feet in height. The line then descended through an alternating series of cuttings and embankments at a gradient of 1 in 85.

It was on this stretch that an embankment fire occurred on 30 July 1943 following the passing of the 4.20 p.m. autotrain from Llangollen. In dry weather, it was not uncommon for sparks from steam locomotives to start lineside fires and on this occasion, some 6 yards of hedge was badly burnt. The owner of the property, a Mr Williams of Maypole Farm, received 15 shillings in damages from the GWR.

The line itself swung through 90 degrees before passing under two road bridges (the latter being the main Llangollen to Ruabon road) before entering Trevor station.

Original Facilities
When the station first opened in 1862, its layout was a very basic affair with just a single platform and station building on the southern side of the running line. Indeed, the mapping of 1875 indicates there to be no passing loop provided; one instead was provided at nearby Acrefair.

The original Welsh name for the district was Chwarele, meaning 'quarry' and the station was originally opened using this name. In his *Gossiping Guide to Wales* in 1882, the author Askew Roberts accounts the observations of English passengers in noting the name Chwarele displayed around the station in its very early years. One passenger remarked: 'I always call places by their right name.' 'Do you,' observed another passenger, pointing to the name on the station board, 'then please tell me the name of this station?' He tried, but the nearest he got to it was 'Gorilla'.

This occurrence was by no means a one-off incident and it seems to have been the cause of so much confusion that the GWR duly set about renaming the station. On 12 June 1869, the *Wrexham Advertiser* recorded:

No. 75023 at Trevor (*Tony Cooke/Colour Rail*)

BR Standard 4MT 4-6-0 No. 75009 brings a two-coach Up service into Trevor on 28 May 1963. The parachute water tank in the yard can be seen on the immediate left, while the station's brick-built signal box can be glimpsed in the background behind the train. (*Tony Cooke/Colour Rail*)

About midway between Ruabon and Llangollen on a branch of the GWR there is a station called Trevor. When the branch was first opened this station was named Chwarele, but as English travellers always despaired of pronouncing the word, the nearest approach to the sound any Saxon was ever known to accomplish being Gorilla, the name was changed to the more mellifluous one of Trevor.

The village around Trevor had expanded rapidly following the opening of the Llangollen Canal in 1805. The production of components for the Pontcysyllte Aqueduct had required the establishment of large-scale industrial manufactories in the area, which were then able to use it to transport their products to new regional and national markets. The exporting of limestone, wrought iron, and bricks became big business, with the beginnings of an important chemical industry taking place at nearby Cefn Mawr in 1867.

In 1862, a private siding owned by J. C. Edwards was constructed from Trevor to his brickworks at Trefynant. Edwards had been born in the area in 1829 and his first venture in clay had been the manufacture of earthenware goods and common bricks. Later, he established works at Trefynant to produce sanitary pipes and firebricks. The railway siding did not stay as such for very long. In 1864, the Pontcysyllte mineral branch was linked to the siding, with the GWR paying Edwards one penny per ton of goods passing over the private line, except for goods coming in or out of his works. Initially, a small fan of sidings was installed to the south of the Vale of Llangollen's line beyond Trevor station.

Improvements

In common with the works being undertaken at nearby Acrefair, major track alterations and station rebuilding were carried out at Trevor between 1897 and 1898. A new station building was constructed on the Down platform, comprising a booking office, parcels office, general waiting room, ladies waiting room, and two lavatories. There was no rear entrance to the station building, so passengers had to use a gateway adjacent to the building to gain access onto the platform and enter from that side.

Passengers wishing to travel towards Ruabon had to cross the line by means of the road bridge, in order to access the new platform. A new waiting shelter was constructed approximately halfway along the Up platform, featuring a general waiting room and urinals. Trevor's platform buildings were built to standard GWR designs, using inlaid patterns of blue glazed facing bricks contrasting with the Ruabon red brick on the rest of each structure.

The formal opening of the new double track through Acrefair and Trevor took place in April 1898; the event was witnessed by some of the directors and other officials of the GWR. By 1910, the GWR had installed a corrugated iron lamp hut at the eastern end of the Down platform adjacent to the road overbridge. This was used to store lamps and lamp oil, plus the tools and spare parts needed for lamp maintenance and repairs.

The expansion of industry around Trevor and along the Pontcysyllte Branch had put a severe strain on the limited goods facilities very early on in the station's history. When the track layout was remodelled as part of the doubling of the line, the GWR took the opportunity to expand the length and number of sidings at Trevor. These were predominantly located on the Down (southern) side of the line. The 1924 GWR report records the three sidings at the Acrefair end of the yard could accommodate sixty-four wagons, while the two at the Llangollen end held thirty-two. A GWR parachute water tank was installed in the yard to service the locomotive shunting there, along with a loading gauge, yard crane, and weighbridge.

In later years, road lorries based at Acrefair would collect containers from the works at Monsanto and convey them to the yard at Trevor. The yard crane would then be used to lift the containers onto 'CONFLAT' railway wagons for onward transportation.

Signalling

By 1884, train movements around Trevor were controlled by a dedicated (albeit rudimentary) signal box to the west of the station's platforms. In addition to the single track main line from Ruabon to Dolgelly (and onwards to Barmouth), two industrial branch lines began at Trevor serving local brickworks. J. C. Edwards' line was originally laid in 1862 as a quarter of a mile private siding to link brickworks at Trefnant with the then newly opened Vale of Llangollen Railway

On 28 May 1963, BR Hawksworth 0-6-0PT No. 1628 busies itself shunting around Trevor yard. (*Tony Cooke/Colour Rail*)

and would become part of the Pontcysyllte mineral branch in 1864. Another private siding to Roberts and Maginnis brickworks trailed off northwards to the west of the station.

Concurrent with the line's doubling between Ruabon and Llangollen, a new thirty-two-lever signal box was ordered in 1897. The lever frame for this originated from Bala Junction when that was enlarged during the same year. Trevor signal box was fitted with a block switch, enabling it to be switched out at quieter times while the line was still open to traffic.

Approaching the station from Ruabon, the view of the Down Home signal was initially restricted to the presence of two road overbridges in quick succession. A repeater signal had been installed to assist locomotive crews to see the signal, but in December 1921, the GWR authorised its recovery and this was duly carried out the following year.

The GWR service timetables for the summer of 1935 show that the Trevor signal box was required to be open from 5.30 a.m. until 6.40 a.m. to accommodate the early morning goods train from Ruabon known as 'The Shooter'. The box could then be closed until 8.05 a.m. with the arrival of the next goods service and would then remain open until 9.30 p.m. There was generally no requirement for the box to be open on Sundays.

Traffic and Trade

From the outset, Trevor's position on the Ruabon to Llangollen section of the line meant that it enjoyed a far more intensive passenger service than the stations further to the west. The GWR Winter timetable of 1877 shows seven services calling at the station towards Ruabon, with a further six towards Llangollen. By contrast, the intermediate stations between Corwen and Bala were only being served by four trains in each direction. Sundays were a very different matter, with three services calling at Trevor towards Ruabon and only two bound towards Llangollen.

Despite the intensity of services, the responsibility of Trevor station rested with the station master at nearby Acrefair. A porter would look after Trevor, dealing with any tickets and parcels as required. Station staff were generally on duty from 6.45 a.m. until 9 p.m. each day. This arrangement meant that when the last passenger services called at the station around 9.30 p.m., it was the responsibility of the guard to extinguish the platform lamps and issue any tickets to the late-night passengers.

Passenger receipts at Trevor were generally lower than Acrefair and reflect the pattern at the other stations on the line. The annual total at the turn of the twentieth century of around 31,000 tickets sold reduced to just over 10,000 in 1933. The number of parcels handled over this period also reflected the trend at Acrefair, when 4,695 were forwarded in 1903, rising to a peak of 5,563 in 1913. Subsequent years saw a decline in parcels traffic and during the 1920s and early 1930s, the figure remained around the 2,700 mark.

Run Down and Closure

The station remained changed little during the line's final years. All the original 1890s structures remained until the day of closure in January 1965.

Following the withdrawal of passenger services, plans were drawn up for Trevor signal box to be taken out of use. The former Down line through the station was to be retained and amendments made to the track layout in order to retain access to sidings. A two-lever ground frame was planned for installation at the western end of the platforms on the formation of the former Up line, controlling access to the McGinnis Siding. An identical lever frame was to be sited to the south of the running line opposite from the signal box, controlling access to the station yard and the Monsanto Chemical Works. Both frames were to be released by a key on the single line staff, in line with an adopted 'one engine in steam' policy. The surviving BR plan for this work is dated August 1965 and certainly by the time an enthusiasts' special visited the line on 17 July no such work had commenced.

During 1965, steam-hauled goods working still passed through Trevor yard on their way to Acrefair (Low Level) and Monsanto's private siding. This was in connection with the removal of waste from Monsanto for subsequent dumping into Birkenhead's Morpeth Dock.

The Pontcysyllte Branch to Monsanto officially on 1 January 1968 but when the branch actually closed is still unknown. Due to weight restrictions, the only locomotives ultimately allowed on the branch were the BR-built 16xx pannier tank locomotives. Possibly, traffic ceased as early as September 1966, when the last 16xx locomotive No. 1628 was withdrawn.

The final track lifting through the station towards Ruabon was completed by May 1969, with all the station buildings being razed to the ground. The platforms themselves remained in situ, becoming sentinels overlooking the empty trackbed. During the early 1990s, the remains of its demolished signal box and water tank base were recovered by the 'Friends of Carrog Station' for use by the preservationists there. Today, the station site has developed into a mature woodland and nature area for the benefit of the local community, although the remains of the brick platform faces can still be identified.

Platform edges at Trevor station, 2012.

Road overbridge at Trevor station, 2012.

The platform edges are still discernible at the former Trevor station site. The western end of the Up platform is pictured here in 2018, standing proudly over the now overgrown trackbed that still sports much of its original ballast.

Wright's Siding (3 m 53 ch)

After departure from Trevor, the line continued its descent into the Dee Valley. Just over 1 mile from the station, the line passed under a minor road at Bryn Howel. Immediately after this bridge was Wright's Siding, which was originally the property of Henry Robertson and was put in to accommodate traffic from limestone quarrying nearby.

A signal box was provided here in order to shorten the section between Trevor and Llangollen. By the time of the 1924 GWR report on the route, the signal box was only being used occasionally and the key for it was kept in Llangollen Station signal box. Consideration was already being given to dispensing with the box, although Wright's Siding still appears in the GWR service timetables of 1935. It was noted that 'the 5.45 a.m. Goods ex-Ruabon will take any traffic for the siding through to Llangollen, to be brought back by the 12.15 p.m. Goods from Corwen, which will also take out any traffic going forward for the siding'. Both the signal box and the siding were removed before the outbreak of the Second World War.

To the south of the line at this point was a large, half-timbered country house built in the late nineteenth century. Now known as the Bryn Howel Hotel, it was originally the family home of J. C. Edwards, who owned quarries, brick and tile works in the area. The railway then crossed over the Llangollen branch of the Shropshire Union Canal before running parallel with it until Sun Bank Halt was reached.

BR Standard 2-6-0 No. 75021 is seen nearing Bryn Howell between Trevor and Sun Bank Halt, with a Chester to Barmouth service on 25 April 1964.

Observed from the third carriage behind the train engine, ex-LMS 2-8-0 No. 48697 approaches Bryn Howell on the return leg of the RCTS 'The Wrexham, Mold and Connah's Quay Railway Rail Tour' on 29 April 1967. (*John Feild*)

Sun Bank Halt (4 m 15 ch)

Significant Dates
Opened to passengers: 24 July 1905
Renamed: 1 July 1906
Closed to passengers: 5 June 1950

Situation
The halt was situated in a truly idyllic spot in the midst of some of the Dee Valley's hidden countryside. Originally known as 'Garth and Sun Bank Halt' when it opened in 1905, the first part of the station's name was dropped the following year. The halt was located on a narrow shelf below the level of the adjoining canal and Ruabon to Llangollen road, overlooking the River Dee. Access was possible opposite the Sun Inn public house, crossing over Bridge No. 41 on the canal, before heading down a short track to reach the halt. A continuation of this track passed over an occupation crossing at the west end of the platforms, giving access to the fields below the railway and a small footbridge across the River Dee, leading to the nearby golf links.

With the ruins of Castel Dinas Bran towering above, the RCTS 'WM&CQ' Rail Tour passes near the site of Sun Bank Halt on 29 April 1967, on its way to Llangollen Goods Junction. (*John Feild*)

Original Facilities

In a bid to attract more passengers to the line, the GWR opened the halt at Sun Bank on 24 July 1905. A basic affair from the outset, its two platforms were 247 feet in length and constructed from wood. A traditional GWR 'pagoda' style shelter made of corrugated iron sheets was installed on each platform. The halt remained unstaffed throughout its existence, with the Llangollen station master supervising it and arranging for the lighting and extinguishing of the platform lamps. Owing to the remoteness and sparsity of the community it served and with no major goods consignors, the station was not provided with any sidings or goods facilities.

Traffic and Trade

Passengers wishing to travel from Sun Bank had to give a clear signal to the engine driver as their train came into sight, usually by holding out their arm in the same way that a bus can be stopped today. Tickets were then bought from the guard on the train, who also collected tickets from those who wished to get off at the halt.

The summer timetable of 1935 reflects the poor passenger usage with just two services calling at the halt towards Llangollen; the 8.25 a.m. Ruabon to Llangollen auto train at 8.38 a.m. and the 2.15 p.m. Wrexham to Llangollen railmotor service at 2.44 p.m. (commenced on 16 September and advertised as running two minutes earlier in the public timetable). For those few passengers heading towards Ruabon, there were two Up services to choose from during weekdays: the 7.30 a.m. Bala to Chester service at 8.30 a.m. and the 3 p.m. Bala to Wrexham mixed service at 4.21 p.m. Interestingly, the first of these Up services was not advertised in the public timetable and would only stop to pick up passengers when required. No services called at the halt on a Sunday.

By the summer timetable of 1938, only the 8.38 a.m. local service to Llangollen and the 4.20 p.m. towards Ruabon remained, with still no service on a Sunday. By the winter of 1947, the service had been reduced even further and only the 8.38 a.m. auto service to Llangollen remained.

Run Down and Closure

Sun Bank Halt was an early casualty, with closure coming on 5 June 1950. The wooden platforms and corrugated waiting shelters were quickly dismantled, although the occupation crossing at the western end remained in use until the line's ultimate closure.

Sun Bank Accident, 1945

While the halt itself may have been unremarkable during its relatively short existence, it has become well-known due to the tragic events of one September morning in the final months of the Second World War.

In the early hours of 7 September 1945, the canal above the railway burst its banks just to the west of Sun Bank Halt. This had drained the canal for a distance of more than four miles, sending all of its water cascading down the embankment towards the railway and resulting in a gap in the trackbed between 100 and 200 feet long. The two sets of rails along with their sleepers remained intact and were left suspended in mid-air. Tragically, the block and telephone wires had not severed, meaning that the signalmen on duty at Trevor and Llangollen Goods Junction signal boxes had no way of knowing about the breach in the track.

The first train of the day along the line was scheduled to be the 3.55 a.m. Chester to Barmouth mail and parcels train. This consisted of a 1921 vintage GWR 'Mogul' type locomotive No. 6315, some sixteen goods wagons and a guard's van at the rear of the train. It was reported that the train was mainly carrying mail for the various towns and villages along the line, the latest newspapers and around £250,000 in cash destined for the local post offices and to pay the wages of the many troops stationed in camps across West Wales.

With driver David Jones and fireman Geoffrey Joy in charge on the footplate and guard Fred Walter Evans inside the brake van, the train passed through Ruabon station at 4.35 a.m. and turned onto the Barmouth line. At 4.47 a.m. the train passed signalman Williams at Trevor signal box, who had sent the message 'train entering section' using his telegraphic instruments to signalman Hall at Llangollen Goods Junction signal box further up the line. The train was by now under 2 miles from the breach.

As the train approached Sun Bank Halt, Joy was leaning out over the left-hand side of the locomotive's cab, watching the isolated lights on the other side of the valley. Jones was seated on the right-hand side of the locomotive, with his hands on the controls, while Evans was sitting inside his GWR 'Toad' brake van writing his reports. In the dark, neither Jones nor Joy was able to see the breach in the track ahead, as the train thundered on towards it at around 35 mph.

The locomotive plunged into the breach, striking the opposite wall and coming to rest more or less upright, buried up to its running plate in the soft earth, with its chimney about 12 feet below rail level. The engine received no serious structural damage though it proved impossible to recover it intact. The tender had remained coupled to the locomotive and was found on its left-hand side. The wrecked underframe of one of the two leading bogie vans was resting on top of the locomotive, behind and above which all of the remaining vehicles were piled up in a tangled mass of wreckage filling the breach. Fire had broken out almost at once, probably from the scattered firebox embers and quickly developed into a blaze, completing the destruction of all the vehicles except for the brake van.

Jones was killed instantly as his side of the locomotive's cab was crushed and when his body was recovered two days later, his hand was found to be gripping the brake handle as if in a final attempt to stop his train running into the breach.

Joy and Evans were far more fortunate, with both having remarkable escapes from the accident. In the case of Joy, it was his position leaning over the locomotive cabside that probably saved his life. Upon impact, he was thrown out of the cab and landed more than 100 feet away, almost buried in mud and falling earth. His recollections were recorded in the summer 1981 edition of the *Steam at Llangollen* magazine:

Waking up feeling cold and wet, and with no memory of what had happened, imagined that he was still in bed and began clutching at imaginary bedclothes to keep warm. Only minutes later did the stark reality of the situation dawn upon him when from the corner of his eyes he saw flames and then realised that he was trapped in mud and earth. He clawed his way out and ran back to the train but there was nothing he could do for the heat would not let him get near enough to the train. Suffering from shock and burns, a broken wrist and a fractured ankle, he began to make his way along the railway towards Llangollen to alert the authorities.

At the rear of the train, Evans had been knocked unconscious by the accident and remembers coming around to the smell of burning wood all around him:

> Through the window of his [brake] van he could see flames and, panic-stricken, he tried in vain to open the door to escape. It would not budge. He then crawled along the steeply sloping floor of the van to a window at the opposite end. He managed to open it and squeezed out of the window only to see all around him the blazing remains of his train. Looking around for a way of escape, he noticed in the light of the flames a broken rail only a few feet above his head. He leapt upwards, grabbed the rail and climbed along it to safety.

Suffering from severe shock, Evans first thought was for the safety of the following train, so began the 2-mile walk back along the line to the Trevor signal box. Upon arrival there, he found that the following train was still being held at the signal and he was duly greeted with 'Why haven't you cleared the section?'

Four fire pumps from Llangollen and Wrexham were deployed to the site to tackle the blaze, using the remaining water in the canal to douse the flames. The fire burnt on for nearly 4.5 hours before it was finally extinguished. Only in the daylight could the full and horrific extent of the accident finally be seen. The breach in the canal bank, the smouldering wreckage of the train, the channel scoured out by the torrent of water and the slurry mixed with goods from the train piled high in the meadow below the line.

Only now could the clear-up operation begin in earnest. The location and topography of the accident site made the process of clearing the wreckage particularly difficult. A 45-ton breakdown crane had arrived on site on the same day, but little progress was made as the crane could not safely get near enough to the breach to make any heavy lifts. In the end, three lorries were anchored in the meadow below the line and the 8-ton pull of their winches was augmented to 32 tons by wire rope tackles and snatch blocks in order to drag the wreckage, piece by piece, sideways out of the breach.

By the evening of Monday 10 September, all the wreckage had been cleared except for GWR 'Mogul' No. 6315. The following day, the boiler, which was practically undamaged except for its fittings, was lifted clear of the engine frames by the crane and the tender was pulled out sideways. After considerable excavation, several unsuccessful attempts were made to lift out the locomotive's frames with the crane, and later to drag them clear with the winches and tackles anchored to the rails. The recovery team was left with no other choice than to scrap the locomotive on site; cutting through the frames between the leading and driving coupled wheels. The two parts were then removed from the breach on Wednesday 12 September, using the power of two winch lorries supplemented by the winch of a bulldozer.

In the meantime, work was underway to repair the railway line across the breach and restore public services as soon as possible. A temporary bridge for the Up line was constructed from the war emergency timber stored at Ruabon. Pile driving commenced on Monday 10 September and the bridge was completed, with the permanent way, by 4 p.m. the following Monday.

It was, however, considered advantageous in the long run to retain the Up line in the engineer's hands until sufficient block stone and ash filling had been tipped from the bridge, enabling the Down line to be restored. Progress was such that a single line train service was instituted over the Up line from the 20th while tipping continued on the Down line. Normal double line working was resumed, under restricted speeds, at 12.15 p.m. on 22 September after a lapse of fifteen days. The superstructure of the temporary bridge was recovered but the piles were left in the bank.

Altogether, approximately 1,900 cubic yards of filling were tipped and in addition, two Royal Artillery bulldozers were used to push back about 3,000 cubic yards of debris from the meadow into which it had been washed by the flood from the canal. Local legend has it that most of the £250,000 being carried on the train was just bulldozed away with the slurry, but the post office vehemently denied this and stated that most of it was, in fact, recovered.

A sylvan view of the 8F-hauled railtour passing near the site of Sun Bank Halt on 29 April 1967, on its way to Llangollen Goods Junction. The placid waters of the River Dee can be seen in the foreground, although as previous years had shown, this was not always so.

4
Llangollen to Corwen

Llangollen (6 m 14 ch)

Significant Dates
Opened to passengers: 8 May 1865
Excursion platforms constructed: 1898
Closed to passengers: 18 January 1965
Closed to goods traffic: 1 April 1968

Situation
Llangollen Station was located 5 miles 40 chains (5.5 miles) from Llangollen Line Junction and was (and indeed still is) a prominent feature of the town. Its location beside the River Dee was both iconic and a restriction to its development over the years. In June 1930, a retired GWR Superintendent recalled Llangollen:

> A favourite inland resort of Welsh people in North Wales and Liverpool.... On Bank Holidays, if wet, people wanted to leave early, if fine the trains were packed. At Llangollen for some years there was but one line of rails for up and down trains, which added to the difficulties. The jovial humour and good natured fun of the crowds were an abiding feature.

However, the town has not always been the popular tourist town being enjoyed by visitors on the GWR's trains. At the end of the seventeenth century, a correspondent reported that there were only seventy houses in the town, while in the later eighteenth century, it was dismissed as 'a small and poor town, seated in a romantic spot'. During his excursions through North Wales in the summers of 1798 and 1801, Reverend William Bingley recalled:

> I wandered into the dirty, ill-built and disagreeable town of Llangollen. The streets are narrow and all the houses are built of the dark shaly stone so common in North

Wales. The situation of this place is, however, truly delightful to the admirer of nature: it stands on rocks that overlook the Dee, and surrounded by high and bold mountains.

Rev. Bingley's visit came at the dawn of some considerable developments that were to transform the fortunes of the town. A branch of the Ellesmere Canal was constructed to the town in 1808, while in 1817, Thomas Telford began surveying the route of a new road from London to Holyhead which would pass through the town. By 1819, the London mail coaches were able to make the journey as far as Bangor in relative safety. The improved transportation links brought with it the development of local industries such as quarrying and wool-working, while the scenery attracted increasing numbers of tourists.

Approaching Llangollen from the east, the line of the new railway skirted through the grounds of the old Vicarage, which later became the Woodlands Hotel. At one time, the old Vicarage was the home of the Jagger family, with their son, Sam, being a keen cricketer. It is said that on his return from matches, Sam would regularly throw his kit bag from the passing train to avoid carrying it back from Llangollen station. Unfortunately, things went awry one evening when he overthrew his bag and it ended up crashing through the window of the parlour where his father was sleeping.

Just west of the Vicarage, the line crossed a private road to flannel mill. A telephone was provided at the crossing and a porter was dispatched with a key from Llangollen station when the gates required opening. There was also a subway for a few cottages alongside the line and a small crossing gate giving access for the Lower Dee Mill's employees. The line then passed alongside a bowling green, which was reached by a footbridge over the tracks from the Ponsonby Arms public house opposite. The line then ran through reverse curves along the bank of the River Dee before passing under Bishop Trevor's road bridge and entering Llangollen station.

Original Facilities

When the extension of the railway westwards from the original Llangollen Vicarage terminus opened in 1865, the new station on the northern bank of the river had not yet been completed. Consequently, the first public passenger train bound for Corwen departed from the temporary station on 8 May was accounted in *The Carnarvon and Denbigh Herald*:

> A special excursion train left Llangollen about noon, filled with a large and fashionable company of friends and well-wishers of the line. Leaving the temporary station of the Vale of Llangollen Railway the train proceeded to the new joint station of the two railways, passing under Llangollen bridge, which, at one time, was considered one of the wonders of Wales.
>
> The toll collector's house having been removed, a new one has been built by the company of cut-stone in the castellated style as a '*tête du pont*'. This, as well as the

several stations on this line we are upon, is built from designs by Mr Pountney Smith of Shrewsbury. In consequence of the unusually severe winter some of the stations have not been completed; but they are all of a very chaste and appropriate character, and very far superior in architectural design to that of railway stations generally.

Having picked up some carriages which had brought down a party of visitors from Corwen, the train proceeded amidst the ringing cheers of throngs of the inhabitants assembled in the neighbourhood, passing on the right the goods station, which has now been open for some little time, and which showed unmistakable evidence of large traffic.

The new station to the west of Bishop Trevor's bridge was constructed on a very commanding site, which also provided a number of challenges when considering the layout of its buildings and platforms. A ramped access road was provided directly from the northern end of the bridge, falling initially at 1 in 426, before steeping to 1 in 92 towards the station.

Pountney Smith's design for the station building was in a similar vein architecturally to his other stone 'hunting lodge' style buildings that were adopted by the Llangollen and Corwen Railway. The biggest difference was that its layout was designed to fit the restricted space available, with the building being generally perpendicular to the platform and running lines. The entrance to the booking hall was originally positioned to face onto the station ramp, with the ticket office being on the right as passengers entered.

No. 48697 is seen rounding the check-railed curves out of Llangollen on the return leg of the RCTS 'The Wrexham, Mold and Connah's Quay Railway Rail Tour' on 29 April 1967.

No. 48697 departing Llangollen, April 1967.

No. 48697 at Llangollen, April 1967.

Originally, Llangollen boasted just one platform on the Up side of the line and the tracks were covered with ash, as was the fashion at the time. A second platform alongside the river was added early on in the station's history, complete with associated gas lighting and a waiting shelter. The shelter is curious in that it was a very ornate yet rudimental affair, constructed opposite the station building and appears to be completely non-standard compared to other structures on the line.

Improvements
By May 1898, work had begun on constructing a footbridge linking the two platforms at Llangollen. The restricted nature of the site resulted in one end of the footbridge being ingeniously cantilevered over the river containment wall. Unfortunately, this did not meet with universal approval from the general public and prompted one anonymous individual to write in to the *Llangollen Advertiser* on 12 May 1898:

> I am very sorry to find that the Great Western Railway Co. are making such an eyesore as a cumbrous and ugly footbridge over the railway at Llangollen Station. Was it originally intended, minus the steps, to convey cattle for auction? The natural beauties of Llangollen bridge and surroundings have been marred. The Cerrig-y-Llan footpath on the opposite side of the river is being beautified, whereas the north side is being spoiled by the Railway Company.

To accommodate the increasing numbers of passengers wishing to visit Llangollen and the surrounding Dee Valley, the GWR embarked on a programme of doubling the line between the town and the main line connection near Ruabon. Progress was such that by Friday, 8 July 1898 the *Llangollen Advertiser* was able to report:

> The additional line, which is being laid at Llangollen Station from the Bridge in the direction of Trevor, was opened for traffic on Sunday, in the presence of a large number of spectators, and regular traffic was commenced upon it on Monday morning, This, together with other station improvements here, at Trevor and Corwen will be appreciably felt in this district.

At Llangollen, modifications were made to the station building to accommodate the new footbridge. This protruded out from the southern gable-end wall above the booking hall and was covered over, providing passengers at least some protection from the elements. The design facilitated access to the footbridge from Abbey Road behind the station via a doorway above the booking office. Initially, it was intended that first-class passengers could use this entrance, with one member of their party (usually a servant) then heading down the stairs to purchase the tickets in the booking hall beneath. Today, the connecting room linking Abbey Road and the footbridge has become the preserved Llangollen Railway's Henry Robertson suite and is used as a meeting room, as well as becoming a venue for wedding ceremonies and temporary museum displays.

Above: Llangollen station, *c.* 1905.

Below: The station's signal box and horse landing are captured on film from an arriving westbound passenger service, *c.* 1963.

The separate waiting rooms and toilet block on the Up excursion platform at Llangollen is seen from a departing westbound passenger service.

The doubling of the line through the station platforms brought with it new requirements for the number of signals, points, and telegraphic equipment needed at Llangollen. To cope, two new signal boxes were built to replace a single earlier box at Llangollen. One of these was built around half a mile west of the station at Llangollen Goods Junction, where the double track section reverted back to being just a single track. Llangollen station's platforms were also extended westwards to cope with lengthy excursion trains. Separate entrance and exit ramps were provided from these so-called 'excursion platforms' up to the Green Lane road bridge. New waiting rooms and lavatories were built halfway along each platform to complement those in the original station building.

In September 1900, the section from Llangollen Line Junction to Llangollen Goods Junction was officially inspected by Major General Hutchinson, who gave the newly laid double track his seal of approval.

Signalling

The station's earliest signalling was at best rudimentary and proved unable to cope with the increasing pressures of excursion traffic. In 1884, a small wooden signal box was erected at the eastern end of the Up platform, adjacent to the horse landing. Upgrading of the signalling system during the doubling of the line led to the construction of a replacement signal box in 1898. This was located in the same footprint as its predecessor but was built in red brick to a standard GWR type 7a design. As with other boxes added around this time, a prominent feature was the blue brick dressings for the quoins, plinth, and window surrounds.

The signal box was fitted with twenty-five levers and a GWR double twist locking frame. By 1924, the signal box 'was only opened for the purpose of dealing with trains attaching or detaching traffic or to facilitate the working of trains at holiday times and in any other exceptional circumstances'.

Owing to the station's awkward position on a sharp curve, track circuits were installed by the GWR in 1898. These enabled the signalman at Llangollen to know the position of an approaching train from either direction. The *Wellington Journal* made special mention of these 'special electrical appliances' in August 1898, which were installed on the authority of the Chester divisional superintendent, Mr G. Grant, and were reputedly 'a unique feature on the Great Western Railway'.

Between 1915 and 1926, the GWR carried out various renewals to the signalling at both Llangollen station box and the nearby Goods Junction box. The work included replacing the Victorian equipment that had been installed including the track circuitry as this had become outdated and non-standard. The *London Daily News* of 14 April 1906 reported a 'Signalman's Amazing Story':

> A dastardly attempt at train wrecking is reported today. Signalman Rowland Ellis Evans, of Corwen, who is stationed at Llangollen to assist in coping with the holiday traffic, was walking along Ruabon Road shortly before eleven last night, when his attention was attracted by noises on the railway line, which runs parallel with the road near Woodlands. Looking over the hedge he saw two men busy laying obstructions across the metals, and knowing the down train was due in quarter of an hour, he got over the fence to investigate. Two men armed with heavy bludgeons closed with him, felling him to the ground and Evans stated that he was struck with a sharp instrument when falling—scars on his throat bearing evidence to this fact.
>
> When he came to himself his assailants had decamped, but heavy obstructions of sleepers and fencing poles lay across the lines. Believing that these were too heavy for him to move, he started full speed for Llangollen along the permanent way, to signal the incoming train to stop. Rushing hurriedly into the signal-box at Llangollen platform, he turned the distant signal at Woodlands at danger. He then remembered that the driver was only instructed to slow up and take care when the distant signal is at danger and ascertaining that the train had left Acrefair. As there was no means of stopping it before reaching the place where the line was blocked, he caught the guard's lantern and, swinging the red light to and fro, dashed off down the line past the obstacles on the metals, towards Trevor.
>
> Succeeding in arresting the attention of the driver of the incoming train, which pulled up a few hundred feet from the danger, Evans then collapsed. Willing hands lifted him into a compartment of the train, which, when the line was cleared, proceeded to Llangollen. There Evans was removed on a stretcher to the waiting room and attended by Dr Williams. Yesterday he was sufficiently recovered to make a statement.

Traffic and Trade

The restrictive space available in the environs of Llangollen station led to the goods facilities being positioned beyond Green Lane road bridge. The yard could be found at a higher elevation to the north of the running lines, with access being obtained through a spur from Llangollen Goods Junction.

At the heart of the yard was the goods shed, which measured 71 feet long and housed two 1-ton cranes. The building was constructed of dark red brick with classical detailing and a slate roof with boarded eaves. The siding through it was capable of holding thirteen wagons and the parallel siding to the south held seventeen. An additional two sidings to the north were each capable of holding twenty-five wagons.

A weighbridge was initially installed alongside the goods shed, but this was subsequently replaced by an upgraded one nearer to the yard entrance and capable of dealing with heavier vehicles. Cattle pens provided specialist holding areas for livestock being transported to and from the town. Surviving traffic receipts indicate that around 300 trucks of livestock were handled at Llangollen each year between 1903 and 1923. A small proportion of this figure would have been handled down at Llangollen's 'horse landing' located down at the passenger station behind the signal box. During the early days of the railway, wealthier passengers would take their horses with them and the landing platform was installed from the outset to accommodate this.

Back in the goods yard, a coal wharf provided specialist facilities for dealing with deliveries of coal and coke. The majority of the ordinary coal came from local pits including Bersham, Gresford, Hafod, and Ifton collieries. Anthracite would be sourced from South Wales, whereas coke came from a range of plants including Shelton near Stoke-on-Trent.

Goods traffic made a significant contribution towards Llangollen's total traffic revenue. Of the total receipts of £18,709 in 1924, £9,572 came from goods, and £1,617 from parcels traffic. Indeed, in the previous year, Llangollen had received 4300 tons of general goods, 6782 tons of coal and coke and 1793 tons of other minerals. From the cattle dock and horse landing, 310 trucks of livestock were handled, while from the station and goods shed combined, 30092 parcels were forwarded on. The record year for parcels traffic appears to have been 1903, when an impressive 33,294 parcels were forwarded on.

It is worth recounting that there are some unfortunate instances of injury and even fatalities throughout Llangollen's railway history. Perhaps the most tragic was the case of a twenty-four-year-old Ruabon man by the name of Hector Leigh who was hurrying to catch a train from the station in May 1924 when he collapsed and died on Llangollen Bridge. It was reported that he had been staying with his fiancé's family in the town over the weekend and was returning home when the sad incident occurred.

However, such instances were generally few and far between when it came to passengers. Railwaymen ran a far greater risk and often it would only take a momentary lapse in concentration to cause serious injury or fatality. In November

The ubiquitous sight of a GWR Pannier Tank locomotive with an autotrain on a Bala to Wrexham service. Collett-designed 54XX No. 5416, built in 1932, was far younger than its two Edwardian-era autocoaches.

1890, ganger James Barrett was engaged oiling some of the points about 50 yards outside of Llangollen station. Aged about sixty, Barrett had considerable experience working on the railways and knew the job in hand and the track layout well. Unfortunately, he did not notice the early morning passenger service leaving the station and was subsequently struck by the locomotive, which severed one of his legs. Barrett sadly died from his injuries a few hours afterwards.

A more curious and still unexplained tragedy occurred in February 1958. With snow still fresh on the ground, the 1.05 p.m. Wrexham to Bala passenger service was on its approach to Llangollen on what had been a quiet and routine journey. The train consisted of a single coach hauled by former GWR '5800' class locomotive No. 5810 (identical to the GWR '1400' class except the lack of push-pull control apparatus required for autotrain working) and was still travelling at around 25 mph. Approaching Factory Crossing, the Croes Newydd footplate crew both had good visibility to the crossing and saw no one standing or walking on it. Due to the curve of the track, the fireman lost sight of it for the last 20 yards but this was expected and would not have come as a surprise to him.

Although not compulsory, the driver sounded the locomotive's whistle as he approached as a precautionary measure. Immediately after the crossing, both men felt the train lurch and quickly applied the brakes to investigate. The fireman and the guard found a body lying about a coach length behind the train, the head and upper portion lying between the rails and the lower part on one side of the track.

At the subsequent enquiry, it became clear that the body was that of a Llangollen station porter who was due to go on duty just fifteen minutes after the incident occurred. Llangollen's station master described how the porter had been sent home the previous day due to a breach of regulations. The enquiry went on to conclude that how the porter got into that fatal situation could only be circumstantial. The absence of any damage to the locomotive's sanding gear and lifeguards ruled out the possibility that he had fallen in front of the approaching train. It was considered possible that the lineside hut adjacent to the crossing had hidden the porter as he walked out into the locomotive or coach, but the injuries sustained would have been more numerous than were found on the body. Sadly, the exact circumstances surrounding the porter's tragic end could not be satisfactorily determined.

Run Down and Closure

Notices advertising the closure of the passenger services on the line were posted in October 1963, with objectors having until 9 December to make their case known. If no objections were forthcoming, the line would close from 6 January 1964 and alternative transport would be provided by Crosville Motor Services.

In December 1963, surviving documentation reveals that a lengthy list of repairs was requested at Llangollen. A detailed inspection had found that four windows in the Booking Office were cracked, with a further five in the booking hall. Dry rot was noted in both the Down side waiting room and gents' toilet, while one of the former's windows was also cracked. On the Up platform, the Louvre windows in the toilets were either black or missing. It is not known whether all these repairs were implemented.

The closure process continued on well into 1964, with the provisional January closure date being missed and a series of consultations taking place. Despite the Transport User's Consultative Committee for Wales and Monmouthshire recommending that closure of the line would cause hardship for the travelling public, the Minister of Transport agreed in September 1964 to close the Ruabon to Barmouth.

A second provisional closure date, 23 November 1964, was missed because the proposed new bus services could not be approved in time. This caused further postponement and the closure date was accordingly moved back to Monday 4 January and then to Monday, 18 January 1965.

However, nature was to have its final impact on proceedings, as on the night of 12–13 December, the line was severely damaged by extensive flooding. At Llangollen, the raging waters of the River Dee engulfed the station and trackbed. All rail services were suspended until the waters subsided, but it was soon discovered that the real damage had been done further down the line near Llandderfel.

Train services were restored between Ruabon and Llangollen from Thursday 17 December, with an emergency Crosville bus service being provided between

Llangollen and Bala. So it was that in this fragmented state that Llangollen station closed to passenger services after Saturday, 16 January 1965, with goods traffic lingering on until 1968.

The final passenger train from Ruabon passed through the platforms in April 1967, in the form of an enthusiasts' special. Organised by the Railway Correspondence and Travel Society, the 'Wrexham, Mold and Connah's Quay Railway Rail Tour' proceeded as far as Llangollen Goods Junction where it terminated and the locomotive (an ex-LMS 8F 2-8-0 No. 48697) ran around the train. Permission was not granted to stop the train in the platforms at Llangollen because the BR management was concerned that it might encourage the International Eisteddfod organisers in their campaign to allow excursion trains to run.

Fortuitously, all of Llangollen's station buildings, signal box, footbridge and platforms survived after the lifting of the track during 1968 and 1969. This would lead to the establishment of a preservation society that has fledged into the Llangollen Railway we know today.

Yet, before preservation efforts commenced in earnest, some items from around the station were destined for re-use on another heritage railway. The large water tank from the Down platform, three water cranes, and the Up starting signal were removed by volunteers from the Severn Valley Railway. The signal has since been installed at their Arley station and is mounted on the Up platform as Signal No. 23. It has even enjoyed a brief appearance on television, when it featured in the plot of the BBC situation comedy *Oh, Doctor Beeching!* during the mid-1990s.

No. 48697 at Llangollen, April 1967.

Berwyn (7 m 60 ch)

Significant Dates
Opened to passengers: 8 May 1865
Downgraded to an unmanned halt: 1956
Closed to passengers: 18 January 1965

Situation
From Llangollen, the line continued for another half a mile before Llangollen Goods Junction was reached. The junction marked the end of the double-track section from Ruabon and the commencement of the single line towards Barmouth. A spur from the goods yard dropped down to meet the main running lines at this point, while another spur headed off in the opposite direction towards Pentrefelin, giving the impression of more double-track.

The line continued to climb at around 1 in 100 as it swung westwards alongside sidings at Pentrefelin. These had been installed to not only handle local slate traffic, but also to accommodate the regular stabling of excursion coaching stock when not required in the platforms at Llangollen station.

Immediately after swinging away from the Pentrefelin sidings, the single-track line crossed over the River Dee by means of a three-span metal skew bridge. The line then hugged the valley side between the main Holyhead Road (the present day A5) and the River Dee as it climbed up the 1-in-80 gradient towards Berwyn.

The steep-sided gorge around Berwyn proved to be a very demanding site on which to build a station. The route of the pre-existing Holyhead road and the course of the Dee had left little room for construction, so like at Llangollen, the station had to have a very small footprint. Despite all this, the substantial station building was built on a ledge on the southern side of the river.

Prior to the arrival of the railway, there was already a small but vibrant community in this part of the valley. A chapel had been built by the Welsh Calvinist Methodists alongside the road in 1848. An enterprising mine owner by the name of Exuperius Pickering had constructed his own chain link bridge, so that he could get consignments of coal over the river and deliver it to Corwen and Bala. Permission for the bridge was granted in 1814 and it opened in 1817 or very soon afterwards. A hotel and inn were located at the northern end of the bridge, dating from 1828 and later rebuilt and extended in a mock-Tudor style.

Original Facilities
Despite the spatial constraints, a substantial station building was built at Berwyn from local brick complete with adjoining accommodation for the station master. Just one short single platform was provided, which would prove to be a challenge for many westbound footplate crews restarting their trains on the 1-in-80 uphill gradient over the years.

In its survey of 1924, the GWR rather optimistically regarded the station as serving a population of about 1000 people, incorporating the villages of Berwyn,

Left: No. 48697 at Llangollen Goods Junction, April 1967.

Below: No. 48697 at Llangollen Goods Junction, 1967.

Llangollen to Corwen

With the enthusiasts swarming around the loco, ex-LMS 8F No. 48697 prepares to run around the RCTS railtour at Llangollen Goods Junction.

Pentrefelin in 1967.

On this occasion (as was the case on many occasions), no passengers are present on the platform as Ivatt Mogul No. 46508 rolls into Berwyn in 1963. The gate at the end of the platform gave access to the path down to the famous Chain Bridge over the river.

Vivod, Llantysilio, Llandynan, and Rhewl. However, it was the influence of the local gentry that was the main reason for the station's existence. The Chairman of the Llangollen and Corwen Railway, Lt Colonel Charles Tottenham resided nearby at Plas Berwyn and an agreement dated 26 August 1861 announced:

> A station to be called The Berwyn Station shall be built in ornamental style and contain a first class waiting room in addition to the general waiting room. All passenger trains shall stop at Berwyn if and when required by the owner or occupier of or visitors to Plas Berwyn mansion.

The station's architect, Samuel Pountney Smith, headed his original drawings for the station in 1864 as a 'design for 2nd class station', but as can be seen, this was anything but second class. The pattern adopted was that of a lodge for a great house, with the adjoining three-storey station master's house being finished in a black and white mock-Tudor style. A coal cellar was installed underneath the house, with deliveries of coal being made by means of a grated coal hole directly from the platform. Although the house came with the job, the station master still had to pay rent to the GWR; in 1924, this would have cost him 7 shillings and sixpence a week.

The station itself consisted of a booking office, general waiting room, a ladies' waiting room (originally the first class waiting room), and two lavatories. The ladies' lavatory was inside the building and accessed through the ladies' waiting room, whereas the gentleman's facility was located outside at the rear of the station, featuring large slate slabs against the roadside wall.

In 1916, reports began to circulate in the local press regarding the theft of money from Berwyn. The station master, Robert Morris, reported that from time to time sums of money had been going missing from the booking office and that he had covered these from his own pocket, as he was obliged to do by the GWR. On 23 June, Morris had received from Paddington the money to pay the platelayers wages and during his absence from the office, £5 was taken.

A Corwen newsboy was arrested and admitted his responsibility for the thefts. He said it was his custom to watch the station master go out from the booking office onto the platform and then he would run in and help himself. He had also on occasions found the shutter of the booking office window unfastened and was then able to reach into the till. £7 was recovered from the boy: the full £5 from the robbery on 23 June and another £2 from previous robberies.

Berwyn station, 2018.

Signalling

Through his 1861 agreement, Lt Colonel Tottenham had the right to stop any train passing through Berwyn for his own benefit. To facilitate this some very tall signals were initially provided, with one towering over the station near the eastern end of the building. By 1905, these had been replaced with more traditional GWR 'lower quadrant' semaphore signals controlled from a small lever frame on the platform. Interestingly the official GWR survey drawing for Berwyn of 1907 incorrectly labels this feature as the 'Bedwyn Ground Frame', confusing the station with one on the GWR's Berks and Hants Line in Wiltshire.

Tottenham's influence extended much further than merely stopping trains at Berwyn as and when he wished. In an agreement dated 1891, it was noted that he had 'for some years past been permitted by the [GWR] Company to place and use a telegraphic instrument in the Berwyn station ... and a wire connecting the same with a telegraphic instrument and bell placed by him at Plas Berwyn'. The agreement enabled direct telegraphic messages to be sent and received from the Tottenham's family home at a time when this kind of arrangement was relatively unheard of. A fee of £1 was due to the GWR every May, which intriguingly was also the same amount that the GWR was paying to Tottenham in rent for the telegraphic wires they had placed across his land above Berwyn Tunnel.

The telegraphic instruments at the station and Plas Berwyn were removed following the termination of the agreement in May 1925. The following year, the GWR agreed to increased rent being paid for the telegraph wires above the tunnel, rising from £1 to £5 and 5 shillings per year. Unsurprisingly, the GWR soon had second thoughts on this arrangement and in a letter dated 1 December 1927 to the then-owner of Plas Berwyn, Major Charles Robert Worsley Tottenham (the grandson of Lt Colonel Charles Tottenham), it was recorded that the GWR now 'find it desirable to place the telegraph wires in a cable through Berwyn Tunnel' and were to terminate their previous agreement within six months.

Improvements

In 1878, a plan was proposed for the construction of a siding at Berwyn, which would have been located to the west of the Rhysgog overbridge. However, given the necessary signalling and locking arrangements, the cost was estimated at £740, 15 shillings and 8 pence, a very large sum at the time. The considered view of the GWR General Manager's office expressed in a letter of 23 September was that 'the additional traffic likely to be brought to the line would not justify the expenditure' and the plan appears to have been quietly dropped.

To cope with the increase in passenger traffic during the summer months, the single platform at Berwyn was extended westwards along the viaduct. Given the lack of available space, the wood-decked platform extension was cantilevered off the southern side of the viaduct, supported by wrought iron frames.

From its opening until at least the mid-1890s, the access path down to the chain bridge crossed over the line at the eastern end of the platform ramp. The crossing here was the scene for a fatal accident just a few days before Christmas in 1896, with the *Manchester Courier and Lancashire General Advertiser* reporting:

> Late on Tuesday evening. Jane Roberts, aged 54, who resided at Tydu, Pentrefelin, Llangollen, was run over by a special train while crossing the line by the level crossing at Berwyn Station. She was killed instantaneously, the base of her skull being completely shattered. Owing to the heavy mails the train was divided, and it was the second part which killed Mrs. Roberts.

As both the number of trains and the popularity of the area continued to increase, the GWR set about removing this crossing and replacing it with a pedestrian underpass. A steep pathway was excavated adjacent to the railway, almost as a continuation of the platform ramp, leading to a 6-foot wide subway under the railway. The structure in its self may have been fairly unremarkable, but for the fact that it was finished in white glazed bricks.

The bricks seemed to have taken pencil markings readily, especially from the indelible type issued to soldiers during the First World War. One surviving message is signed by R. Roberts in July 1913. Next to it and dated 25 December 1914 is written Lance Corporal R. Roberts, suggesting that he had enlisted, been promoted and had returned for Christmas on leave. A partially obscured note, signed by A. J. Candy, reads 'I really want—is baby'. Sadly, an Alfred James Candy is honoured on Llangollen's War Memorial (unveiled by Captain Best of Vivod on 8 July 1923) as having fallen in action.

In modern society, graffiti is rightly seen as defacement and vandalism in most situations. Yet, after the passage of a century, the written messages on the subway walls have become poignant and important historical artefacts in their own right. What is even more remarkable is that the messages have survived at all, following the period of disuse and neglect when the railway through Berwyn was closed and dismantled. The *Shrewsbury Chronicle* of 14 February 1868 reported a 'Fatal Accident':

> On Friday evening, as the 5-45 train was leaving Berwyn Station, a country woman named Margaret Hughes of Glyndyfrdwy, met with an accident which caused instantaneous death. It seems that she had travelled by this train for some distance and intended going to Acrefair, but got out at Berwyn in order to transact business with a man in another carriage. The train was in motion before she returned to her compartment. She, however, tried to open the door and rush in, but was dragged some yards, knocked down, and instantly killed. The station master rushed to her assistance immediately he saw her lay hold of the carriage door, but he was dragged some yards, hurled on the platform, and hurt in the face and other parts. An inquest was held at the waiting room in Berwyn Station, on Monday, before B. H. Thelwal Esq., and a verdict of 'Accidental Death' was found. This is the first accident of this nature which has occurred on this line since its opening.

A view from the train on 22 June 1963 showing the historic Chain Bridge over the River Dee. The adjacent hotel has since been much enlarged and continues to prove popular with visitors to the area.

A view of the Chain Bridge Hotel prior to its extensions during the early 1960s, viewed from the bottom of the railway embankment.

Run Down and Closure
When the line had become nationalised, the task of supplying anything from brooms and dusters to timetable posters and furniture remained with the stores department based at the former Great Western Railway's works at Swindon. On 31 March 1953, a new bench seat was dispatched from Swindon for use at Berwyn and arrived by goods train.

However, in common with other stations on the line, the 1950s and 1960s saw contractions in an effort to make the line pay. These efficiency savings resulted in the downgrading of Berwyn into an unstaffed halt in 1956, with the station facilities being reduced to just a small wooden waiting shelter on the platform. The timber platform extension over the viaduct was becoming life-expired and due for replacement, so this too was removed. In a final act of ignominy was the attachment of a small board emblazoned 'HALT' to the underside of the station's running-in board on the shortened platform.

After its downgrading, Berwyn still continued to receive some attention from railway staff, albeit on a very occasional basis. As late as July 1964, a request was sent to the Llangollen station master for attention to the spring on the gate at Berwyn, in a bid to stop sheep 'straying off the road'. A wall lamp case fastener also required attention, although it is unclear whether these repairs were actually carried out.

Deeside Loop (9 m 36 ch)

The long 5-mile section between Llangollen Goods Junction and Glyndyfrdwy must have caused many delays on busy days. For westbound trains, the ruling gradient of 1 in 80 from the Dee Bridge eased only to 1 in 135 through the narrow confines of Berwyn Tunnel, before finally levelling out. A heavy goods train could take over fifteen minutes to pass through the section, delaying faster passenger services and causing having havoc with the single line schedules. It was an obvious candidate for improvements, so in 1908, GWR commenced construction of a passing loop on a level section of the line to the west of Berwyn Tunnel in order to break up the single-track section.

Crossing loops other than at stations were not common on the GWR's network and it is worth studying Deeside Loop in some detail. The loop line was located on the northern side of the main running line and could accommodate a train of forty-five standard wagons. A signal box was installed approximately halfway along the passing loop on the Down side to control movements and oversee token exchanges between trains.

Deeside Loop signal box was a standard GWR wooden-type design measuring 21 feet 2 inches by 12 feet 1 inch and was accessed only by a footpath from the nearby A5. An eighteen-lever frame was installed within the signal box, of which five levers remained spare. Deeside Loop could be 'switched-out' when not required, returning it back to a long section between Llangollen Goods Junction and Glyndyfrdwy. Trains would then use the Down loop line (the original running line) in both directions.

The signal box was usually only required during the day and the signalman was included with the Glyndyfrdwy staff. By the summer of 1935, Deeside Loop signal box was open between 7.45 a.m. and 3.45 p.m. during the week and did not open at all on Sundays.

However, by the mid-1950s, the general decline in rail traffic meant that the passing loop and signal box were not being required as often as previously. During the summer period of 1956, only one train a week was scheduled to cross with another at Deeside Loop; these were the 12.30 p.m. Saturdays only Birkenhead to Barmouth service passing the 11.10 a.m. Pwllheli to Birmingham Snow Hill at 2.28 p.m. Accordingly, the box was closed on 15 March 1964 and the loop recovered.

After leaving the loop behind, the line followed the course of the River Dee westwards towards the village of Glyndyfrdwy. This section of the line was also one of the more isolated and did not share the valley with the main A5 road, as this climbed over the hills to the south before converging again in Glyndyfrdwy at a higher level.

Glyndyfrdwy (11 m 32 ch)

Significant Dates
Opened to passengers: 8 May 1865
Goods facilities withdrawn: 4 May 1964
Closed to passengers: 18 January 1965

Situation
The small village of Glyndyfrdwy had its fortunes transformed by the arrival of the railway and the concurrent growth of the slate quarries around it. The station was constructed on the northern fringes of the village and was reached by a steep minor road down from the main A5. This road passed over the railway by means of a gated level crossing before continuing northwards and bridging the River Dee to connect to the old drovers' road between Corwen and Llangollen along the northern side of the Dee Valley.

Original Facilities
When it first opened in 1865, Glyndyfrdwy boasted a single stone platform and running line was graced by a fine station building. As at Berwyn and Carrog stations, Pountney Smith's elegant design aimed to replicate a lodge on a grand estate. The public entrance to the station was through the rear-facing doors which led into the general waiting room. Prospective passengers would have found the booking office and associated ticket hatch on their left-hand side, while a first-class waiting room was located behind a sturdy wooden door on their right.

Train crossing facilities were neither provided nor required by the simple timetable then in operation. The opening timetable for the railway in May

Glyndyfrdwy GWR luggage label.

Glyndyfrdwy station viewed from the Corwen end of the Down platform, with the level crossing gates firmly closed across the line on 28 September 1959.

1865 indicates just three departures towards Llangollen on weekdays and four towards Corwen.

A substantial two-storey house for the station master was provided at the western end of the building. The height of the stone wall surrounding the house's garden afforded some privacy for the station master and his family. For the majority of the station's Victorian history, the station master at Glyndyfrdwy was Hugh Eastick, who was first recorded as living in the station house in 1871 aged twenty-eight. Twenty years later, Eastick was still in residence and was being described as 'Station Inspector'. By 1901, the position of station master had transferred to the wonderfully named Christmas Roberts who brought up five children with his GWR salary. *The Shrewsbury Journal* of 25 June 1884 reported a 'Sad Bathing Fatality':

> A sad bathing fatality occurred in the river Dee, in the Vale of Llangollen, on Friday evening. A railway porter named Thomas Burgess, employed at Glyndyfrdwy Station on the Great Western Railway, was bathing in the Dee in company with two others, during the interval between the trains. In wading across the river Burgess got into a deep hole; the Dee being very treacherous in many parts. The other men hastened to rescue their drowning companion, but one of them was eagerly clutched and dragged down the stream. A desperate struggle ensued and it was feared both would be drowned. The scene was witnessed by several persons on the banks of the river, who made efforts to save the drowning man. After a severe struggle Burgess released his companion who perished, the other man being ultimately rescued.

Signalling

The construction of the second platform and passing loop at the station in 1877 resulted in the opening of a signal box to control train movements and the adjacent level crossing. The GWR's major modernisation programme of the line's signalling in 1897 led to the ordering of a new signal box for Glyndyfrdwy. This was located on the Up platform opposite the main station building and was built in a very similar style to that at Carrog. The wooden gates protecting the level crossing were operated by a wheel inside the main signal box.

A twenty-five-lever frame provided enough capacity to control the majority of the station's trackwork and signals, with lever No. 5 being spare. A two-lever ground frame controlled access to the two sidings on the Llangollen side of the level crossing and was housed in a dedicated wooden hut. The frame could be unlocked by the key kept on the electric train staff for the section.

The position of Glyndyfrdwy's signal box alongside the level crossing required it to be operational whenever trains were running. The GWR service timetables for the summer of 1935 show that the box was to be opened by 4.15 a.m. on weekdays and Saturdays and would then remain so until 11.30 p.m. On Sundays the box was only required for two brief spells: from 11.15 a.m. until 11.55 a.m. and then from 8.30 p.m. until 9.05 p.m. The weekday and Saturday opening times remained the same during the winter of 1946–47, but by that stage, there was no requirement for Sunday opening.

An undated view of the signal box and waiting room at Glyndyfrdwy station.

Traffic and Trade

Before the arrival of the railway in 1865, quarrying and agriculture were the main sources of employment within the village. Small scale extraction of local stone for building and stonewalling was already taking place. From the 1840s, the nearby slab quarry had been producing sills, doorsteps and slabs for flooring as well as field and boundary posts.

The new railway produced a boom in slate and slab extraction in the valley, with Glyndyfrdwy briefly at its centre. The transformation in fortunes is perhaps best exemplified by local resident Edward Philips. He was recorded as 'farmer' in the census of 1851, becoming a 'timber merchant' by 1861 and finally a 'quarry manager' in 1871.

In order to transport the slate away from the quarry site, a narrow-gauge tramway was completed in November 1877, linking in with the standard gauge line at an exchange wharf. The following month, the GWR agreed to lay a connecting siding to the east of Glyndyfrdwy station, with the slate being transferred between narrow and standard gauge wagons by means of an overhead gantry crane. This transhipment arrangement was destined to continue well into the 1940s.

As with many other rural stations along the line, goods traffic revenue at Glyndyfrdwy was over twice that from passenger ticket sales in 1924. Indeed, in the previous year, Glyndyfrdwy had received 142 tons of general goods, 653 tons of coal and coke, and 286 tons of other minerals. With the absence of a cattle dock, no livestock was handled, but over 1,200 parcels were forwarded on from the station. The record year for parcels traffic appears to have been just before the outbreak of the First World War, when 2,578 parcels were forwarded on in 1913. The *Gloucester Citizen* of 30 June 1923 reported a 'Cruel Way of Sending Puppies by Train':

> At Corwen Police-court on Friday, Thomas Davies, farmer, Bethania, Cardigan, was fined 50 shillings for sending two sheep dog puppies in a small starch box a long distance by rail to Glyndyfrdwy Station. A constable said the dogs were pressed down in the box, in which they could not stand upright and the lid nailed over them. One has died since from this cruel treatment.

Run Down and Closure

Goods facilities at Glyndyfrdwy lingered on until 4 May 1964, in line with the general withdrawal of goods facilities from the majority of the other intermediate stations. The signal box and passing loop survived in use right up until the last trains departed on the night of 12 December 1964. For the final few weeks of operation, the station building remained staffed and open to issue tickets to passengers travelling on the replacement bus service.

The track remained in situ for some time after closure, while the Government reconsidered its transport policy but there was to be no reprieve. Demolition contractors removed the track and the majority of the station's infrastructure

BR Standard 4-6-0 No. 75026 has just passed Glyndyfrdwy's Up Distant signal as it heads the 10.20 a.m. Barmouth to Birkenhead service on 25 April 1964.

including the signal box and Up waiting shelter. The main station building and adjoining station house were sold off as a private dwelling and the remainder of the site grassed over. Part of the station site became a children's playground for the benefit of the local community. The long and challenging process of reviving the railway lay ahead.

Carrog (13 m 41 ch)

Significant Dates
Opened to passengers: 8 May 1865
Closed to goods traffic: 4 May 1964
Last passenger service by rail: 12 December 1964
Closed to passengers: 18 January 1965

Situation
Upon departure from Glyndyfrdwy, the line ran right along the bank of the River Dee before taking a meandering route westward. It remained within sight of both the A5 main road to the south and River Dee to the north until reaching the outskirts of Carrog. The route benefitted from a very gentle climb, with gradients ranging between 1 in 737, stiffening slightly to 1 in 352.

The line passed the foot of Glyndwr's Mount, which is a tree-covered mound that is reputed to be the site of the Welsh patriot Owain Glyndwr's house, from where Glyndwr raised his standard in a revolt against the English in Wales in September 1400. In February 1915, a section of the Mount slipped across the railway and into the river. A large gang of men with picks and shovels were drafted in to carry out remedial work to stabilise the bank.

Facilities
Carrog's position within the wide Dee Valley afforded the railway company the space to construct the station in the most convenient layout possible. The western end of the station was located alongside the B5437 road, which linked the Holyhead Road with the village of Carrog. The station building is to a similar design to that at Glyndyfrdwy but located on the northern side of the line rather than the latter's southern position.

The building incorporated a booking office, general waiting room, and first-class waiting room (latterly the ladies' waiting room) with its own lavatory. As was the case at Glyndyfrdwy, a house for the station master was an integral part of the building. At the time of opening, the building was 'of a very chase and appropriate character, and very far superior in architectural design to that of railway stations generally'.

The construction date of the Down platform presents something of a mystery, as it has not been possible to determine whether it was built in 1865 or during later Victorian improvements. It is considered likely that the platform was installed

Viewed from the adjacent road bridge, the overall layout of Carrog station can be seen to good effect on 28 September 1959. Carrog's camping coach, once a regular feature of many country stations, can be seen in the yard.

during the mid-1890s when capacity improvements were being made and new signalling installed. The waiting shelter was constructed to the universal GWR design of 'Ruabon red' and blue bricks with a Welsh slate roof. Internally the shelter consisted of a warm and cosy general waiting room, with outside urinals on the eastern end. Access to this platform was either by means of a barrow crossing or using the road overbridge at the Corwen end of the station.

The 1924 survey of the entire route records the station staff as comprising one station master and two porter signalmen. The station master would have paid a rental of 3 shillings and 9 pence per week to the GWR for the use of the station house, which was handily inclusive of rates.

Signalling

During the major signalling infrastructure upgrade of 1897, a new platform mounted signal box was constructed on Carrog's Up platform. This housed a nineteen-lever frame to control all movements around the station and into the goods yard. In 1907, 'switching out' equipment was installed and it is believed that Carrog was the first location on a GWR single track line to receive such instruments.

When the signal box was switched in, token equipment covered the sections to Glyndyfrdwy in the east and Corwen East in the west. When switched out, the section was extended to cover the entire 5-mile route from Glyndyfrdwy to Corwen East.

The GWR service timetables for the summer of 1935 show that Carrog signal box was required to be open from 10 a.m. until 10.45 a.m., then from 12.10 p.m. until 1.35 p.m. The box could then be closed until 2.30 p.m. and would then remain open for a third spell until 6 p.m. There was generally no requirement for the box to be open on Sundays.

By contrast, the GWR service timetables for the winter of 1946–47 shows that the box only needed to be open for two brief spells per day, rather than the previous three. When required, the box needed to be open between 7.40 a.m. until 9 a.m. and then from 2.20 p.m. until 7 p.m. Again, there was no requirement for Sunday opening.

Trade

The goods yard at Carrog was located on the Up side behind the station's signal box. This consisted of two sidings accessed from the Ruabon end of the passing loop. The most northerly of these sidings could accommodate a maximum of twenty wagons, which in later years would be the location of a popular camping coach. The No. 2 siding could accommodate a further twenty-five wagons and was provided with a horse landing and cattle pens. On the original plans for the station, a disc turntable for wagons is shown in the yard, but this appears to have never been constructed.

Livestock was the principal goods traffic being handled throughout the station's history, although a wide range of items was typically handled. A weighbridge was installed within the yard to assist with the weighing of carts and lorries arriving and leaving the yard.

A small goods warehouse was provided on the Up platform between the station building and the cattle pens. This corrugated sheet structure would have been used as a traders' store for the collection and delivery of goods to and from local traders.

Run Down and Closure

The scheduling of services to cross at Carrog had noticeably reduced by the early 1960s, partially due to excursion traffic being routed away from the Ruabon to Barmouth line. The station's signal box was the first casualty and closed on 23 March 1964. The loop line through the Down platform was closed and lifted at around the same time.

An air of neglect began to descend upon what had previously been a picturesque and immaculate station. The handling of goods traffic ceased from 4 May 1964 and the station saw out its final months in a forlorn state. As with other intermediate stations on the Llangollen to Bala Junction section, Carrog saw its last passenger trains on the evening of 12 December 1964. After this date, the booking office remained open to issue tickets to passengers now travelling on the replacement bus service until final closure took effect on 18 January 1965.

The remains of the former loop at Carrog can be seen as No. 46508 departs the station towards the west. Today, the station has seen a change in fortune, thanks to the efforts of the preserved Llangollen Railway.

No account of the station's closure would be complete without briefly mentioning the painstaking effort and almost Herculaneum task that then commenced to restore the station back to its former glory. The station house had become adopted by Glyndwr District Council as a council house, while the adjoining public part of the building began to deteriorate but was largely complete. The corrugated sheds and the signal box were demolished, while the Down platform waiting shelter became vandalised. Without its slate roof and lead flashing to protect it from the weather, the shelter ultimately collapsed.

In 1989, the station was put up for sale and salvation came in the form of Martin Christie, a Llangollen Railway Society member and mechanical engineer from nearby Cynwyd. The long and exhausting process of bringing the station back to life then commenced, incorporating many surviving items from along the Ruabon to Barmouth line. That the station can once again be enjoyed by so many visitors today is a testament to the vision and efforts of both Martin and the many 'Friends of Carrog' past and present.

Bonwm Halt (14 m 67 ch)

Significant Dates
Opened to passengers: 21 September 1935
Closed to passengers: 18 January 1965

Situation
Beyond Carrog station, the line became a single-track section once more after it passed under the B5437 road overbridge and followed the general contour of the valley, never straying far from the River Dee. Carrog slate siding was passed on the southern side of the line just under 1 mile on from the station. This was initially a private siding, with a key on the electric train staff unlocking the ground frame. A two-foot gauge tramway, linking the Penarth Quarry with a transhipment wharf alongside this siding, was opened by 1868 and lasted until the 1930s. Around half a mile further on from the slate siding, the small unstaffed halt of Bonwm was reached.

By the late 1920s and 1930s, the GWR was experiencing increased competition from road transport. In an attempt to increase passenger numbers on the line, Bonwm Halt was opened between Carrog and Corwen on 21 September 1935, with its name being taken from a small hamlet nearby. The unstaffed halt was located alongside the main Holyhead Road (A5) and a connecting gate was provided between the two.

Original Facilities
Throughout its relatively short existence, the halt at Bonwm was a very basic affair on the southern side of the line. It was constructed with an edging of redundant sleepers with clinker infill and had a platform length of just over 70 feet. Like many other halts of the period, Bonwm was provided with a small wooden shelter complete with electric interior light which was switched on and off by the passenger train guards as required. Official GWR records from October 1935 report the cost of the halt's construction to have been £141.

Traffic and Trade
Special instructions were issued by the GWR to enable the guard's compartment to stop on the platform for any passengers wishing to board or alight at Bonwm. Much skill was also required by the locomotive drivers to achieve this. Guards were initially responsible for selling tickets from the halt to either Corwen or Carrog, from where passengers would then be rebooked onwards to their chosen destination. Passengers leaving the train at Bonwm would have had their tickets collected by the guard.

The summer timetable of 1936 shows six trains in each direction calling at the station during the week, although there was no Sunday service. Prospective passengers heading towards Llangollen in the morning had the option of the 7.54 a.m. and 9.22 a.m. services, with an additional 11.17 a.m. service operating on Saturdays only. For passengers heading towards Corwen, there was a longer wait involved as the first scheduled train to call at the halt was not until 12.39 p.m.

5
Corwen to Bala Junction

Corwen (16m 24ch)

Significant Dates
Opened to passengers: 1865
Closed to goods traffic: 2 November 1964
Last passenger service by rail: 12 December 1964
Closed to passengers: 18 January 1965

Situation
The line approached the town of Corwen on a long, sweeping embankment to provide some protection from the flood waters of the nearby River Dee. The former Denbigh, Ruthin and Corwen Railway's line swung in from the north and ran parallel with it for the last quarter of a mile. This gave the impression of a double-track section, although in reality the two lines were bidirectional and operated independently of each other where possible. A scissor crossover at the eastern end of Corwen station platforms provided access to either platform from each line.

The first appearance of the place-name appears to have been Cornain in 1206 and a year later as Coruain. The modern form of Corwen is documented for the first time in the mid-fifteenth century. The main core of the town had been established on a low river terrace on the southern side of the River Dee.

By the early nineteenth century, the population stood at around 2,000 and many were still involved with cottage industries such as straw-bonnet making, stocking knitters and watchmaking. All of these activities were to suffer a severe decline following the arrival of the railway, bringing with it the availability of mass-produced goods from further afield. Indeed, the railways ultimately consigned some townsfolk to poverty at a time when the only relief was the town's workhouse. However, the railway also became Corwen's biggest employer and

Ivatt 2-6-2T No.41241 is observed off the eastern end of Corwen's Down platform as it arrives with a three-coach train.

Croes Newydd Standard Class 4MT 4-6-0 No. 75029 working a three-coach train comprised of three ex-LMS coaches awaits departure from Corwen station. The train's position along the Up platform suggests that the footplate crew have been taking advantage of the water column here.

A second view of No. 75029 at Corwen, this time viewed towards the west, shows the fireman hard at work, pushing coal down onto the tender flap-plate while the tender's water tank was being topped up.

even as early as 1871, around fifty people are referred to as being either directly or indirectly employed by the railway.

Facilities

Corwen station featured a handsome stone-built single-storey station building on the Down platform and was built to a design by Samuel Pountney Smith. Passengers approaching the station building from the Holyhead Road would have originally passed through well-tended gardens in the forecourt area; these were removed by the GWR in 1929 at the cost of £175 and replaced by a car park.

The main station building a booking hall, booking office, parcels office, station master's office, district inspector's office, guards' room, general waiting room, ladies' waiting room, refreshment rooms, various store rooms, and two lavatories.

From the outset, the refreshment rooms at Corwen were privately owned and the rent paid directly to the GWR. It has become apparent that some confusion had arisen at the GWR's estate office by the summer of 1867, regarding the tenancy agreement and even the name of the tenant. An official letter was subsequently despatched, which read as follows:

> I do not clearly understand … from what date the tenancy of the above Rooms actually commenced. You state in your letter that it commenced on the 26 July 1867 but I think this can hardly be the case as you received and accounted to this

Company for £75, a year and a half's rent, sent in June last. Will you be good enough to give me more precise information as to the date? It seems to me that the tenancy must have commenced at least as far back as Christmas 1865 if not proven. Will you also be good enough to say whether the tenant's name is spelt Moltby or Maltby?

The writing on many items of paperwork from this period is not always easy to decipher. Indeed, some pieces were so illegible that they provoked complaints from railway staff. In 1877, one guard on the Ruabon to Dolgelly line wrote 'Can this be Berwyn? Please instruct Paddington to write more plain'.

The same problem cannot be said for hardware items of railway property such as posters, signs and furniture, which were usually emblazoned with the legend 'Great Western Railway'. Towards the end of the Victorian era, crockery was being produced and used bearing the name of Corwen Station, so that light-handed customers in the refreshment room were not tempted to take items with them. The name of the manufacturer (J. W. Plack) was also displayed on the crockery, Plack being the proprietor of the nearby Crown Hotel at that time.

Like many other important stations, Corwen possessed a bookstall, operated by Wymans. During the late Victorian and Edwardian eras, copies of local maps, postcards, newspapers, and magazines would have been available to purchase from this stall. A popular item at the time would have been the *Navy and Army Illustrated*, an early kind of glossy magazine that mixed shots of military parades and smart soldiers in their uniforms with enticing images of the exotic far corners of the Empire. It was, of course, a subtle means of recruitment to the armed forces, but a particularly effective one nonetheless.

Passengers on the Down platform were protected from the elements by a canopy which featured an unusual ridge and furrow formation. An enclosed footbridge linked the two platforms, although the corrugated sheet cover and windows for this were removed between 1953 and 1957. On the Up platform, a smart red-brick building contained a general waiting room, ladies' waiting room, and two lavatories.

The station also boasted an adjoining road motor garage built of corrugated iron sheet, from where the GWR-operated road motor services as a feeder for the trains. In this respect, the GWR was a very forward-thinking company, and the Corwen operation could be seen as a precursor to the modern 'interchanges' between the road and rail networks.

Signalling

As the whole station site was over half a mile in length, two signal boxes were ultimately provided to control train movements. The line through the station between Corwen East signal box and Corwen West signal box was worked under double line absolute block regulations.

Corwen East signal box was located on the Up platform and controlled the platform area and access to the eastern end of the station's goods yard. The box was opened in 1897 and contained a thirty-five-lever frame. Being at the convergence of the routes from Ruthin and Llangollen, the box featured two different systems to control train movements. For trains using the Ruthin line, there was an electric train staff connection with the next station at Gwyddelwern, as well as a connection with the Denbigh District telephone circuit. For trains using the line towards Llangollen, the box had an electric train station connection with Carrog when that station was 'switched in' to the circuit, and key token equipment with Glyndyfrdwy when Carrog was 'switched out'.

The signal box at Corwen East replaced an earlier platform-mounted version on the Down side, beyond the station's footbridge. The wooden structure was then converted to an office for the GWR's signal and telegraph department.

Corwen West signal box was located close to the A5 overbridge at the western end of the goods yard. It too had opened in 1897 and contained a twenty-five-lever frame. The box controlled entry to the goods yard as well as the single line onwards to Llandrillo, which was worked by electric train staff. A setting down post for the single-line token was located 21 yards away on the Bala side of the box—a picking up post not being required for Up workings due to the double track into Corwen station.

Most Down trains took water at Corwen as exemplified by this view of No.46509 at the head of a Barmouth-bound train, *c.* 1963. The standard GWR design footbridge had by this point lost its corrugated sheet cover and windows.

Above and below: Nos 9017 and 9021 at Corwen, April 1958.

A lone gentleman looks on from the road bridge as BR Standard Class 4MT No. 75023 arrives with the 7.50 a.m. Birkenhead to Pwllheli train on 28 May 1963. Access to the Up platform was by means of the flight of wooden steps visible to the left of the locomotive. (*Tony Cooke/ Colour Rail*)

Traffic and Trade

The goods yard was located at the western end of the station and straddled the running lines. On the Up side, there were five sidings which could accommodate a maximum of 100 wagons. A further two known as 'West End' could accommodate twenty-eight wagons in No. 1 siding and ten wagons in No. 2 siding. On the Down side of the line, there were another five sidings, accommodating a maximum of 115 wagons.

The goods yard was kept busy and at the heart of it was the stone-built goods shed. This impressive structure could house four wagons for loading and unloading at any one time and was purposefully built adjacent to the main Holyhead Road. Inside two cranes were each capable of lifting loads of 3 tons.

One of the more unusual aspects of the goods yard was the Brooke Bond tea hut, which was raised up on pillars to keep out the rodent population and protect the valuable contents during times of flood. The history of Brooke Bond dates back to 1869, when an Arthur Brooke opened a shop in Manchester selling tea, coffee, and sugar. He traded as 'Brooke, Bond and Co.' although there was never any involvement from a Mr Bond as Brooke simply liked the sound of the name. Trade depression in the 1870s forced Brooke to pursue just the wholesale side of his business and by 1897 it was claimed that two million Brits drank Brooke Bond tea every day.

As can be expected for a busy market town, traffic receipts record a very healthy flow of goods and passengers through Corwen. In 1924, goods traffic revenue was about twice that from passenger ticket sales. Indeed, in the previous year, Corwen had received 3,154 tons of general goods, 4,830 tons of coal and coke, and 4,669 tons of other minerals. From the cattle dock, 918 trucks of livestock were handled, while from the station and goods shed combined, 9,715 parcels were forwarded on. The record year for parcels traffic appears to have been 1933, when an astonishing 22,479 parcels were forwarded on.

Such was Corwen's geographical and operational importance as a railway junction that there was originally a two-road engine shed provided at the western end of the goods yard. This was located behind Corwen West box and there were typically seven sets of men based at the shed. Their work extended to Wrexham, Blaenau Ffestiniog, and Barmouth Junction but generally concentrated on the section between Bala and Ruabon.

In 1901, the shed had an allocation of six 0-4-2 type tank engines and seven 0-6-0 type saddle tanks. All the steam locomotives were GWR owned, although the shed facilities were joint GWR/LNWR property. The GWR took the decision to close the shed in 1927, which had implications for the three sets of LMS locomotive crews who were also based there at the time. The LMS ceased to use the shed from 6 August 1928 and its men transferred to Denbigh. The shed building was demolished a short time later, but the shed road and turntable remained in use until the mid-1950s.

Corwen station goods shed, 2014.

Run Down and Closure

Corwen ceased to be a junction for passengers in February 1953, when services to Ruthin ended. However, special 'Land Cruise' trains had been introduced over the line in 1951 as part of the Festival of Britain and were instantly popular. The trains themselves took many different forms over the years but generally involved a circular route around North Wales, taking in Rhyl, Denbigh, Corwen, Bala, Barmouth, Criccieth, Caernarfon, Bangor, and Llandudno Junction.

The year 1961 marked the final full year of these land cruise specials and on Sunday 22 October, the Stephenson Locomotive Society organised a farewell rail tour to mark the forthcoming full closure of the Ruthin to Corwen line the following April. The 'North Wales Rail Tour—Farewell to the Corwen Line' ran from Chester to Corwen via Denbigh and was formed of a 6-car diesel multiple unit.

Like the majority of other stations on the Ruabon to Barmouth route, goods traffic ceased at Corwen from 2 November 1964. The last passenger trains called on 12 December, with the station booking office remaining open until the official closure day the following January. Tickets were still issued but passengers were forced to use the replacement bus service between Llangollen and Bala. The station's refreshment rooms remained open for some time after closure and lasted until at least July 1966.

Diesel multiple units (DMUs) were not common sights on the line, but on 22 October 1961, a six-car DMU stands at Corwen having just arrived via Denbigh with a 'Farewell to the Corwen Line' railtour.

The Ffestiniog Railway Society special headed by BR Standard 4MT 4-6-0 Nos 75009 and 75023 await departure from Corwen on 25 April 1964.

A second view of the Ffestiniog Railway Society special taken from the station's footbridge, with BR Standard 4MT 4-6-0 Nos 75009 and 75023 awaiting departure from Corwen on 25 April 1964.

Llangar Crossing (17 m 35 ch)

On leaving Corwen station, the line passed between the complex of sidings on either side of the main running lines before passing Corwen West signal box and diving under the main A5 road. The railway then took the easy route towards the south-west, striding out across the floodplain of the River Dee in long straight lengths. About half a mile out from Corwen, a minor road was crossed at Llangar near to an ancient church. Llangar Crossing was looked after by a crossing keeper who resided in a small cottage adjacent to the level crossing. The road was frequently used by farmers as it gave access to a large number of fields in the valley.

The crossing was provided with block indicators which were located within the cottage, giving the crossing keeper advance warning of any approaching trains. In 1927, the crossing was attended by the wife of a lengthsman, who received the princely sum of four shillings per week for her duties. Ironically, two shillings and sixpence of this was deducted by the GWR for rent of the cottage. There was no supply of running water to the cottage, so it became common practice for water to be dropped off in churns by goods trains. Despite its proximity to Corwen, the crossing came under the supervision of the Cynwyd station master.

Llangar Old Parish Church itself is worthy of note in that it has been described as 'one of the greatest church wonders of Wales'. Generally abandoned following the building of a new church in Cynwyd in the 1850s, the church was only being used for burials by the 1870s. This turn of events preserved it as a time-capsule from the period without any later alterations and modernisation. Consequently, the church retains many of its ancient features, including fifteenth-century wall paintings, seventeenth-century beams, pews, and a minstrels' gallery.

In April 1873, Llangar Crossing was the scene of a local fatality, when a Mr Robert Owen of Ty'n y Wern was accidentally run over by a train while on his way to Cynwyd station. Given the relatively easy gradients in this stretch of the line, it is unlikely that the locomotive was working hard, further hampering

After passing Llangar Crossing, the line continued climbing gently along its raised embankment towards the village of Cynwyd. The substantial four-span stone Pont Dyfrdwy bridge that carries a minor road over the River Dee came into view on the approach to Cynwyd, with the railway passing under the road at the eastern side of the river bridge. Pont Dyfrdwy is said to date from 1612 and is assumed to be the structure recorded by Welsh botanist Edward Lhuyd (1659–1709) at the end of the seventeenth century. It is similar in style to other nearby bridges across the River Dee, such as Pont Carrog (built 1661) and Pont Cysyllte (1697), which indicates that it too was built during the seventeenth century.

Cynwyd (18 m 30 ch)

Significant Dates
Opened to passengers: 16 July 1866
Closed to goods traffic: 4 May 1964
Last passenger service by rail: 12 December 1964
Closed to passengers: 18 January 1965

Situation
The small village of Cynwyd had grown up on the eastern flank of the valley, at a point where a tributary of the river, the Afon Trystion, had etched a sharp notch down the western slopes of the Berwyn Mountains. Like many of its neighbours, Cynwyd was totally dependent on agriculture and tiny cottage industries and developed as a centre for flannel manufacture in the area. Even after the coming of the railway, the village had just 197 residents in 1901.

The railway station was opened just a short walk down from the village, alongside the banks of the river. This part of the upper Dee Valley was prone to flooding each year and the Corwen and Bala Railway took this into account when constructing the line. The station and railway either side of it were constructed on embankments high enough to combat any floodwaters.

There are no passengers waiting for the approaching train at Cynwyd but hopefully, someone will alight to make the stop worthwhile. The GWR did consider installing a loop and second platform at Cynwyd but the plans were not implemented.

Facilities

In contrast to the country lodge style designs of the intermediate stations along the L&CR, the passenger facilities provided along the Corwen and Bala Railway were far more simplistic affairs. At Cynwyd, the station possessed only one platform, some 347 feet long located on the eastern side of the running line (nearest the village). A single-storey brick building was provided incorporating a booking office, general waiting room, ladies' waiting room, and two lavatories. There were no doors into the station from the village side of the building, with access only possible from the platform side.

The building was a slightly enlarged version of a standard GWR design, with the toilet windows on the eastern gable wall being fitted with louvres. A short canopy extended out over part of the platform but would have afforded little protection to passengers. A notable feature was the inlaid patterns of blue glazed facing bricks around the groins and the arches of its doorways and windows, contrasting with the red exterior bricks on the rest of the structure. On the northern gable of the station, the toilet windows were fitted with louvres.

From the 1880s, a diamond shaped plate with letter 'T' was displayed on the exterior of the building facing onto the platform outside the booking office. This was used to visually indicate the status of the station's telegraphic equipment to crews of passing trains. When working correctly, then a white letter on a black background would be displayed; if faulty, then a red letter on a white background would be shown. This information would then be passed on by the crew at the next large station and the telegraph engineer would be summoned to attend to the fault. The use of these plates on the line lasted until telephone links were installed, generally before 1914.

For the station master, a house was provided by the GWR in Cynwyd village, though the rent for this was deducted from his wages. During the Edwardian era, the green-fingered station master cultivated the area around the station to provide some greenery, with a small garden planted alongside the running line.

The GWR did give some consideration to installing a passing loop and second platform at Cynwyd, but this seems to have been deemed financially unviable and the plan was subsequently shelved.

It can be argued that Cynwyd was actually better equipped to handle goods traffic than it was for passengers. A small goods yard was provided at the southern end of the platforms, consisting of a small loop with headshunts at either end. The central part of the loop traversed the 36-foot-long goods shed, which was built of coursed masonry in a similar style to that provided at Corwen. The sidings in the yard could accommodate twenty-eight wagons if required.

Traffic and Trade

The dominance of goods revenue for the majority of the railway's existence was as true at Cynwyd as it was nationally. Across Britain, goods overtook passenger takings as early as 1852. Indeed, it became common knowledge among railwaymen that goods provided the bread and butter, passengers the jam.

Ivatt Mogul No. 46508 coasts to a stop in the platform at Cynwyd with a Down passenger service. The 6C on the smokebox door shows the loco's allocation to Croes Newydd shed in Wrexham, while the 'SC' below this denotes that No. 46508 has been fitted with a self-cleaning smokebox.

Cynwyd station, 1959.

Such was the local demand; Cynwyd was the first village station on the line westwards from Ruabon to have its own dedicated goods shed. In practice, when a goods train called at Cynwyd, any railway wagons would be uncoupled and left inside the goods shed. A member of the station staff, usually the porter, would examine the corresponding invoices that had been dropped off by the guard or delivered separately by passenger train and then notify the customer either by post or, in later years, by telephone that their goods had arrived.

In the meantime, the goods, if they were part loads—known as 'smalls' (less than a wagonload)—or were perishable or fragile, would have been unloaded onto the platform of the goods shed to await collection. The customer would then arrive with a cart (or, from the 1920s, a lorry or van), deal with the paperwork in the office, and draw up to the platform before loading up. The procedure was reversed with goods being sent from the yard to other destinations.

As with many other stations along the line, a weighbridge was installed in the yard at Cynwyd. Weighing the carts and lorries arriving and leaving the yard allowed the GWR to correctly measure the weight of the loads being conveyed. In 1923 alone, Cynwyd received 308 tons of general goods, 360 tons of coal and coke, and 94 tons of other minerals. From the station's small cattle dock, 146 trucks of livestock were handled, while from the station and goods shed, 1284 parcels were forwarded on. Indeed, during the early 1900s, it was necessary to employ an 'outside porter', whose responsibility it was to collect and deliver items from the local area on behalf of the GWR.

Despite the relatively small size of the village it served, Cynwyd enjoyed a fairly intensive passenger service for such a rural country station. The GWR 1902 timetable shows the following six Up services calling at Cynwyd bound towards Corwen and Ruabon at 8.11 a.m., 9.46 a.m., 11.41 a.m., 4.10 p.m., 5.26 p.m., and 8.44 p.m. during the week. In the Down direction, there were four corresponding services towards Bala and Dolgelley at 8.55 a.m., 10.35 a.m., 5.13 p.m., and 8 p.m., with an additional service at 3.58 p.m. calling to set down passengers 'on notice being given by the passenger to the guard at Ruabon'. Sundays were a different matter, with just one Up service calling at 8.12 p.m. bound for Ruabon, with no corresponding Down service.

The introduction of steam railmotors on the Wrexham to Bala route in 1905 brought a great improvement to the passenger service being offered. The railmotors in essence involved permanently fitting a small vertical-boilered steam locomotive inside one end of a railway carriage, with a driver's compartment at the other. The advantage of this was that it could be driven from either end and time was not wasted by having to reposition the locomotive after arrival at its destination. Despite their initial success, the railmotors were later superseded by autotrains and conventional locomotive-hauled stock around the time of the First World War.

The GWR summer timetable of 1938 shows seven trains in each direction calling at the station during the week, with no service on a Sunday. On some summer Saturdays, a procession of extra trains catering for holidaymakers would have been seen passing non-stop through the station heading to and from the resorts on the Cambrian Coast. The *Liverpool Daily Post* of 4 October 1939 reported a 'Railway Warehouse Fire':

> Llangollen Fire Brigade and Rhug Hall (Corwen) Fire Brigade, together with railwaymen, yesterday fought a fire for several hours at Cynwyd G.W.R. goods warehouse. The cause of the fire is believed to have been a spark from a railway engine, which set the roof of the building ablaze. The fire was got under control, and the warehouse was cleared of goods, which were undamaged.

Signalling

The sidings at Cynwyd were controlled by two small ground-frames, East and West, which were locked by the key on the Corwen to Llandrillo single-line staff. It is believed that a small signal box existed at the station in 1890, although there is no record of it after 1898.

Run Down and Closure

The general run down in trade along the line was first felt at Cynwyd between 1960 and 1963, with the partial demolition of the goods shed. By July 1963, the outer wall of the goods shed and part of the roof had been removed, leaving the line through the shed flanked only by the remains of the wall footings on one side and the loading bay platform on the other. In this denuded state, the station lingered on until the final passenger train passed through in December 1964.

Llandrillo (21 m 6 ch)

Significant Dates

Opened to passengers: 16 July 1866
Closed to goods traffic: 2 November 1964
Last passenger service by rail: 12 December 1964
Closed to passengers: 18 January 1965

Situation

Beyond Cynwyd, the line was practically level and followed the broad valley of the River Dee. Just over 2.5 miles south-west lies the village of Llandrillo. which was served by a far more substantial station than its neighbour. Local legend has it that St Trillo in his wanderings founded a church sometime in the late sixth century, near where the rivers Ceidiog and Dee meet.

By the time the railway arrived in the 1860s, the population of Llandrillo appears to have been around 700 and despite its relatively small size, it had become an important trading centre. The village boasted at least two bakers, five grocers and general dealers, alongside smiths, wheelwrights, joiners and tinmen. There was also a thriving fair held on 25 February, 3 May, 5 July, 28 August, and

Hawksworth Pannier 0-6-0 No. 1663, delivered new to Wellington in 1955, approaches the bay platform at Ruabon with a substantial goods train on 14 July 1964. The track layout, turntable, and sidings on the Down side of the running lines can be seen to good effect.

14 November, which brought in a regular influx of animals and traders. By 1901, the village's population was 648, falling to 532 in 1961.

Facilities

Due to topographical constraints, the railway station serving Llandrillo was located around three-quarters of a mile away from the village centre. When the Corwen and Bala Railway opened its first stretch in 1866, their line terminated at Llandrillo and it was to be a further two years before the section onwards to Bala was completed. A small, attractive, brick building was provided on the Down (south-eastern) side of the line, comprising a booking office, general waiting room, first-class waiting room (latterly a ladies' waiting room), and two lavatories. The building lacked a rear entrance, causing passengers to enter from the platform-facing side.

Llandrillo was provided with a crossing loop and a second platform on the Up side was constructed. A small waiting shelter similar to those provided at Acrefair, Trevor, Glyndyfrdwy, and Carrog was provided on this platform, containing a waiting room and urinals. In the absence of a footbridge, passengers bound towards Ruabon had to use a foot crossing in front of the station's signal box.

Initially, no accommodation for the station master had been provided by the Corwen and Bala Railway; it was expected that he should live locally. In 1898, the

Llandrillo Station looking east towards Corwen in 1959. The small waiting room on the Up platform provided some shelter for passengers and was of similar design to those found at Carrog, Glyndyfrdwy, Trevor, and Acrefair.

Steam is available in abundance to the crew of Ivatt Mogul No. 46508 as they prepare to call at a seemingly deserted Llandrillo station on 28 May 1963. (*Tony Cooke/Colour Rail*)

Great Western Railway incorporated the construction of a new station masters' house at Llandrillo into their improvement package for the line. This resulted in a substantial two-storey building being erected in the yard area behind the Down platform. Unfortunately, the GWR appear to have forgotten to notify the relevant authorities prior to commencing the building work, prompting calls for them to explain their omission publicly.

Surviving photographic evidence for the station interiors along the line is minimal, verging on non-existent in many cases, but this is not the case at Llandrillo. After nationalisation in 1948, the interior of the waiting room appears to have been rather sparse for the ordinary passenger. Wooden bench seating was provided within the white-painted room, with a GWR fusee clock hung on one wall. The ticket office window was adorned with several small enamel signs offering luggage insurance products and making clear that the 'British Railways General Bye-Laws were available for inspection at this booking office'. Handbills detailing the latest services and excursions were hung on strings above the window, with lighting being provided by wall-mounted oil lamps.

The railway staff employed at Llandrillo consisted of a station maser and two signalmen. Initially, a porter from Cynwyd attended to the station's oil lamps, but in later years, this duty fell to the staff at Llanwychllyn station, nearly 11 miles away.

Traffic and Trade

Llandrillo was a railhead for many of the small villages and outlying farms in the vicinity and thus dealt with a wide range of goods throughout its history. Agricultural traffic and livestock remained important sources of revenue throughout much of the station's history, particularly when the regular fairs were being held. These were held in the High Street and in a field below the church and seem to have ceased in the late-Edwardian era.

To handle this traffic, a large goods shed was constructed adjacent to the Down running line and was similar in design to that found at Cynwyd. The stone-built shed measured 36 feet in length, with a two-storey office located at one end. The sidings in the station yard could accommodate sixty-three wagons if required. The siding nearest to the station platform served a cattle dock, while a crane with a lifting capacity of 1 ton was provided in the yard.

Traffic receipts record a very healthy flow of goods and passengers through Llandrillo. In 1924, goods traffic revenue was about twice that from passenger ticket sales. Indeed, in the previous year, Llandrillo had received 548 tons of general goods, 603 tons of coal and coke, and 300 tons of other minerals. From the station's small cattle dock, 226 trucks of livestock were handled, while from the station and goods shed combined, 2,666 parcels were forwarded on. The record year for parcels traffic appears to have been 1913, when an impressive 4,705 parcels were forwarded on.

Wherever parcels and goods were being handled, there was always the temptation for some of it to go 'awry'. As early as 1867, there were local reports of a double-barrelled gun being stolen at Llandrillo while in transit. The culprit, a GWR employee by the name of Alfred Allen, was jointly identified by the station master, Mr Roberts, and Peter Hughes who had allegedly bought the gun from Allen. The *Montgomery County Times and Shropshire and Mid-Wales Advertiser* of 14 July 1894 reported on a 'Shocking Accident':

> A shocking accident occurred on Monday on the Great Western Railway at Llandrillo, near Bala. While the 5 p.m. passenger train was approaching Llandrillo Station, the fireman mounted the tender of the engine to inspect the injector, and in going under a bridge he was knocked off the engine and killed on the spot.

Signalling

Train movements were controlled by Llandrillo signal box, located on the Down platform adjacent to the main station building. This was of the standard hip-roofed brick variety and contained a twenty-five-lever frame. The box dated from February 1897 and was a replacement for an earlier structure which had been in operation between 1890 and 1897. As at Carrog, token setting-down and picking-up posts were conveniently located alongside the signal box in both directions.

Prior to around 1926, the entrance to the goods yard was controlled by a ground frame at the Ruabon end, which was locked by a key on the Llandrillo to Corwen single-line staff. Alterations were affected, enabling the signal box to assume control of all the trackwork and the ground frame was subsequently removed.

The two signalmen employed at the station worked alternate shifts. In the summer of 1935, the signal box was required to be open by 4.50 a.m. and remain so until 10.50 p.m. during weekdays and Saturdays. On Sundays, the box was only required to be open for two short periods from 11.40 a.m. until 12.10 p.m. and then from 8.10 p.m. until 8.45 p.m.

Run Down and Closure

Goods facilities were withdrawn from Llandrillo and the other stations between Bala and Llangollen Goods Junction still handling goods traffic in November 1964. On the night of 12–13 December, floods breached line near Llandderfel and an emergency Crosville bus service was introduced on Monday 14 December between Llangollen and Bala. The station at Llandrillo remained open to issue tickets for passengers using the bus service.

On 25 June 1968, BR's demolition contractors Thomas W. Ward Ltd of Sheffield started work by severing the line at a point between Cynwyd and Llandrillo. Track lifting commenced between Llandrillo and Llandderfel on 2 July. Fortunately, the station masters' house at Llandrillo was retained and now survives as a private residence.

Llandderfel (23 m 62 ch)

Significant Dates
Opened to passengers: 1 April 1868
Closed to goods traffic: 2 November 1964
Last passenger service by rail: 12 December 1964
Closed to passengers: 18 January 1965

Situation
On leaving Llandrillo, the line passed under a minor lane before crossing the Dee on a substantial steel girder bridge. The bridge had received new diagonal bracing to its girders in 1931 and was renewed in 1957, just eight years before the line was closed. Now on the northern side of the River Dee for the first time since Pentrefelin (Llangollen), the line continued towards the small village of Llandderfel.

About halfway between Llandrillo and Llandderfel was the private Crogen Halt or 'Shooting Platform' as it was sometimes known. This had been installed specifically for Henry Robertson, who owned the large country house of Crogen on the opposite side of the river. As had been the case with Tottenham at Berwyn, Robertson was granted the privilege to stop any passenger train he wished to at Crogen, for the benefit of himself or any of his visitors. The halt consisted of a 66-foot-long platform and was devoid of any shelter or building.

Indeed, Crogen Halt never appeared in any of the public timetables and appears to have been used only occasionally by Robertson prior to his relocation to the nearby Palé Hall. Beyond the Halt, the line resumed on an embankment before crossing back over the River Dee on a two-span girder bridge at Dol-y-Gadfa.

Original Facilities
Situated just over 23 miles from Llangollen Line Junction, the station at Llandderfel originally opened in 1868 and served four small settlements, of which its namesake was the largest and closest. Originally, the station boasted just a single platform with a building similar to that at Llandrillo. The building comprised a booking office, general waiting room, first-class waiting room (later to become the ladies' waiting room), two lavatories, and a separate coalhouse and lamp room.

At the western end of the station, a gracefully arched bridge carried the B4401 Bala to Llandrillo road over the line. Llandderfel was overlooked by the Bryntirion Inn, a small public house and hotel. The main entrance to Palé Hall was located across the road from the station. The Hall was reputed to be one of the finest Victorian houses in Wales and was the private residence of Henry Robertson, and later his son Henry Beyer Robertson.

The railway staff employed at Llandderfel consisted of a station master and two signalmen. Initially, a porter from Cynwyd attended to the station's oil lamps, but in later years, this duty fell to the staff at Llanwychllyn station.

Some of the original drawings showing the opulent interior of Pale Hall.

Improvements by Royal Appointment

In a letter from the general manager's office on 9 July 1889, it was announced that the platform at Llanderfel was to be extended to accommodate the visit of Queen Victoria to North Wales. To allow for the LNWR Royal Train, it would need to be of at least 420 feet in length, so it was decided that a permanent addition of 240 feet would be added at the eastern (Ruabon) end. A temporary extension of 250 feet was constructed to the western (Bala) end, which would include a narrow section underneath the road bridge. The total cost of the work was estimated to be £200.

A grand awning was erected around the station building to provide some extra cover for the distinguished visitors. Every conceivable preparation was taken by the time the Royal Train steamed into Llandderfel just six weeks later. The Queen arrived from her Osborne summer residence on the Isle of Wight at 8 a.m. on Friday 23 August, accompanied by Princess Alice, Princess Beatrice, and her husband Prince Henry of Battenberg. They were welcomed on the heavily decorated platform by numerous local dignitaries and were presented with a 'magnificent bouquet in the form of a Welsh lyre [stringed musical instrument]. The Queen was unfatigued but leant heavily on her stick. Her Indian retainers aroused great curiosity'.

The Royal party then proceeded on to Palé Hall by road as guests of Henry Beyer Robertson and used it as their base for their five-day visit. On the Saturday afternoon, the Royals drove back to Llandderfel station and boarded their train at 3.30 p.m. bound for Ruabon, from where they toured to Ruabon and Wrexham by road, before returning by train from Wrexham at around 6 p.m.

On the Monday morning, the Prince and the two Princesses visited a colliery in Ruabon, descending into the pit and 'firing a shot' to blast the coal. The miners assembled at the pit's mouth to give them a hearty cheer as the Royals drove away. In the afternoon, the entire Royal Party proceeded to Llangollen by train, before driving to the home of Sir Theodore and Lady Martin at Bryntysilio near Berwyn for afternoon tea. This was not without incident, as when the train entered Llangollen station, a gentleman by the name of David Thomas threw himself on to the rails. He was knocked down and severely injured; the wheels of the steam locomotive passed over his legs and one of his arms. Thomas was removed to the nearby cottage hospital where he died two days later.

The Tuesday saw the Royals splitting up to make the most of their final day in North Wales. The Queen spent the day at Palé Hall and met the Llandderfel village choir, while Princess Beatrice and Prince Henry proceeded out to Barmouth to lay the foundation stone of a new church there. At around 10 p.m., the party departed Palé for Llandderfel station, from where they boarded the Royal Train for their long journey onwards to Balmoral.

Improvements in the 1890s

When news of Sir Henry Beyer Robertson and his new wife Lady Robertson reached Llandderfel that they were due to return from their honeymoon in December 1890, a public meeting was held in the village school. The tenants of the estate and local parishioners discussed the best way to celebrate the occasion. The centre of attention was naturally the railway station; where Sir Henry and Lady Robertson were due to arrive back by special train.

The station was elaborately decorated, with the walk from the train being carpeted at the expense of the station master, Mr J. Roberts, who also assisted a Mr Robinson with the decoration of the station canopy. The *Wellington Journal* of Saturday, 31 August 1889 reported:

> Festoons of evergreens were conspicuously hung along its top and Chinese lanterns of various colours and sizes added to the appearance of the whole surroundings. In the verandah were artificial rhododendrons, which in the flickering glare occasioned by the light of the lanterns, the moon overhead and the lighted torches, presented a very cheerful appearance.

Around 1897, a new platform and passing loop were installed on the southern side of the station. A waiting shelter was installed on the newly constructed platform, to the standard GWR design of red and blue brick with a Welsh slate roof. The building contained a small waiting room heated by a traditional coal fire, with urinals located separately on the eastern end.

This period at the end of the Victorian era marked the zenith of the railway locally, as the village's population soon began to fall from 912 in 1901 to just 659 by 1961.

Signalling

Between 1890 and 1897, the station boasted a small signal box, but this was replaced by a larger brick version on the Up platform. The new box featured a fourteen-lever frame and its position commanded a view of approaching trains from either direction. The box controlled all the passing loop points, point locks, and the signals, but not the access to the goods yard, this being operated by a small ground frame locked by the key token.

The GWR nameplate ordering register from the Edwardian era records that a plate spelt 'Llandderfel' was ordered on the 16 November 1908. This presumably was a replacement for the single 'D' version originally affixed to the front of the signal box.

The GWR service timetables for the summer of 1935 show that Llandderfel signal box was required to be open from 4.55 a.m. until 10.45 p.m. during weekdays and Saturdays. On Sundays, the timetabling required the box to be open for two thirty-minute intervals: from 11.45 a.m. until 12.15 p.m. and then from 8.05 p.m. until 8.35 p.m.

It was normal practice on single track railways to sound the locomotive's whistle when approaching distant signals. However, this requirement did not apply to trains approaching Llandderfel's Up Distant signal. The close proximity of the signal to Palé Hall meant that a treadle was instead fitted to the track, which sounded a bell in the signal box to warn of the approaching train. That way, no whistling was required and the residents of the Hall remained undisturbed.

Traffic and Trade

At a lower level than the Up platform, a small goods yard was installed to serve the needs of the local communities and Palé Hall. The yard featured two sidings, with No. 1 siding capable of accommodating thirty-one wagons and No. 2 siding holding a further eighteen. A goods warehouse was located halfway along No. 2 siding and featured a 1-ton capacity crane for the handling of more cumbersome consignments. At the end of the siding could be found the cattle pens, where livestock was held prior to onwards transportation by road or rail.

Any wagons destined for Llandderfel were detached from the train and, under the supervision of the station master, were allowed to roll into the yard by gravity alone. Great skill was needed to apply the handbrakes in the correct manner to stop the wagon where it was needed in the yard.

Unlike at many of the other stations along the line, goods traffic was generally far less of a revenue stream than passenger traffic. Indeed, in 1924, passenger receipts were double the goods receipts. In the previous year, Llandderfel received only 283 tons of general goods, 442 tons of coal and coke, and 297 tons of other minerals. From the cattle dock, just forty-one trucks of livestock were handled. Parcels traffic remained quite important throughout the station's history, with 3,677 being forwarded on in 1903 alone.

Run Down and Closure

Tom Thomas was the signalman on duty at Llandderfel on the night of 12 December 1964. After seeing the last train through the station (the 9.40 p.m. Wrexham to Bala passenger service), Thomas locked up the box and headed for home, little knowing that this would be the last time the box would be operational. The River Dee was already in flood and he had to wade waist deep along the road to reach his home in the village.

Daybreak brought the news that a section of railway embankment near Dol-y-Gadfa Farm had been completely washed away. The decision was taken to suspend services on the Llangollen to Bala section, resulting in the premature closure of the railway through Llandderfel.

When track lifting finally commenced, it took place either side of the breach, with gangs commencing works eastbound and westbound. Track lifting commenced between Llandderfel station and its Down distant signal on 2 July 1968. Remarkably, all of the buildings at the station remained in situ until at least July 1978, although the windows and internal fittings had long since been removed.

This stay of execution was not destined to last and all the buildings were finally razed by February 1980. Redevelopment of the station site was on the cards, with the intention of constructing a series of holiday cottages. Building work did commence on several of these but was never completed and one unfinished bungalow remains to this day surrounded by the encroaching woodland. The steps from the B4401 roadway down to the Up platform still survive as a reminder of the long-lost railway here.

In the spring of 1993, a party of volunteers restoring Carrog station visited the site to recover the remaining GWR spearhead railings. After a hard day's work, these were transported back to Carrog and have since been repaired and erected along platforms 1 and 2 there.

Llandderfel Tunnel

Midway between Llandderfel and Bala junction the line passed through a rocky outcrop, which resulted in the construction of the 157-yard-long Llandderfel Tunnel. This was brick lined at each end, but the central section remained as bare rock.

In May 1879, the tunnel became the scene of an audacious escape for one local prisoner being conveyed from Bala to Ruthin Gaol. Just as their train was approaching the tunnel, John Williams asked the accompanying policeman Thomas Jones to release one of his hands from his handcuffs on the plea that they were hurting him. No sooner had Jones complied with his request when the prisoner dealt Williams a blow with the handcuffs and made his escape through the carriage window. A search of the tunnel and lineside was made but no trace of Williams could be found. Unfortunately, Williams' plan backfired as it appears he injured his right foot while jumping from the train. A month later, he was recaptured in Wrexham and was transported to Ruthin Gaol without further incident.

Bala Junction (27 m 16 ch)

Significant Dates
Opened to passengers: 1882
Last passenger service by rail: 16 January 1965
Closed to passengers: 18 January 1965

Situation and Facilities

First seriously mooted by Colonel Tottenham in 1860, a railway linking the slate quarries of Ffestiniog to the lakeside town of Bala came to fruition in 1882. Single track for most of its length and running through the wild and difficult terrain, the new railway provided a station at Bala far closer to the town centre than would otherwise have been the case. Yet, providing a small Welsh town with more convenient access to the railway network was merely a fortunate by-product of a far more ambitious project by the Great Western Railway. The prize was independent access to the slate industry around Blaenau Ffestiniog, with the GWR providing the most direct route to the Midlands and beyond to London. If Blaenau Ffestiniog was the 'town that roofed the world', the GWR aimed to provide the main artery despatching this precious cargo far and wide.

The new line joined the Corwen and Bala Railway at a point to the eastern end of Bala Lake. In 1880, a new Bala Junction station was constructed purely as an interchange between the two lines. It would become one of only two junction stations in Wales not to appear in the public timetables; the other was Pontsticill in South Wales.

The original layout at Bala Junction consisted of an island platform, with the Down line towards Dolgelly and Barmouth being on the south side and the Up line towards Ruabon being on the north. The line from Blaenau Ffestiniog and Bala Town ran in from the western end to join the Up line.

However, the increase in traffic on both lines led to Bala Junction becoming something of a bottleneck and the layout was changed considerably in 1884 to cope. A new platform was installed to the south of the station, connected to the Down line by a long loop. The island platform was retained and another loop installed on the northern side.

An elegant footbridge linked the island platform with the Down platform to the south. This featured the interwoven GWR monogram in its gusset plates, with the date of 1884 also being incorporated. A connecting footpath near to the footbridge on the Down platform gave access to the station from the nearby golf course. No vehicular access was ever provided.

Given its position alongside the River Dee, the station enjoyed a plentiful supply of water. Originally there were four water-columns installed to replenish the tenders and tanks of steam locomotives using the station. These were reduced to three during the 1950s and were all fed from a water tank near the signal box. It would be easy to assume that water was pumped from the river, but this was not the case as a water main linking into the mains supply at Bala had been installed. Thirsty passengers were accommodated through the installation of a public tap at the western end of the island platform, complete with an accompanying 'drinking water' sign.

In the summer of 1896, the local councils began discussions on whether the station at Bala Junction should be done away with altogether. The Bala Urban Council 'believed that everyone was ready to admit that Bala Junction was a great inconvenience to passengers' and even called a special meeting in mid-August to discuss the matter. A resolution was drawn up and sent out to all the surrounding councils to drum up further support. In October, the Dolgelly Urban Council joined in support and wrote to the GWR requesting that they do away with the station at Bala Junction and run all trains to Bala (Town) instead. All such requests seem to have been very politely turned down by the GWR.

Signalling

Originally, the signal box controlling movements around Bala Junction was located on the south side of the station, adjacent to the Down running line. The remodelling of the track layout in 1884 resulted in a new signal box being erected on the north side. This originally housed a twenty-eight-lever frame, which served until 1897 when the signal box was substantially extended on its eastern side. A fifty-three-lever frame was installed making Bala Junction the largest box on the line. The original lever frame was transported to Trevor for use in the newly built signal box there.

The GWR service timetables for the summer of 1935 show that Bala Junction signal box was required to be open from 5.05 a.m. until 11 p.m. during weekdays and Saturdays. On Sundays, there were only two brief spells when the box needed to be open: from 11 a.m. until 12.55 p.m. and then from 7.55 p.m. until 8.30 p.m.

An overall view from the western end of Bala Junction station in 1959. In the foreground is a milepost indicating that the station is 26 miles 40 chains from Llangollen Line Junction.

LMS Standard Class 2MT 2-6-0 No. 46509 awaits departure from Bala Junction with a working towards Ruabon.

Proving the accuracy of the station's signage, a passenger at Bala Junction samples the drinking water available, *c.* 1963. Behind him is the water crane, drainage funnel, and the chimney of the brazier, which was used to heat the water column in times of frost.

The GWR Moguls were at one stage a regular sight on the Ruabon to Barmouth line before the introduction of Ivatt Mogul and BR Standard designs. One such example is No. 5344, built to a Churchward design at Swindon in 1918 and seen approaching Bala Junction with a Land Cruise service. No. 5344 was destined to have a working life of forty years; being withdrawn from Taunton shed in 1958 and subsequently scrapped.

Taken from the line-side, the crew of BR Standard 4-6-0 No. 75024 have certainly got a free steaming locomotive as they prepare to leave Bala Junction with an Up passenger service on 5 May 1964. The main Down platform on the left was rarely used. (*M. Beckett/Colour Rail*)

Run Down and Closure

When the section from Bala Junction to Llangollen was closed due to flood damage in December 1964, trains from Barmouth were brought into the station before reversing to reach Bala station. Ironically, this was exactly the situation that the local Victorian councils had been calling for back in the 1890s.

In the summer of 1968, the signal and telegraph department of the preserved Ffestiniog Railway gained permission from the BR Signals Department at Reading to remove any redundant signalling equipment from around Bala Junction. Vehicular access was not possible given the station's remote location, so the volunteers assembled a platelayer's trolley at a spot a quarter of a mile to the west and used this to assist with the operation.

The timber post signals were found to be in excellent condition, with a slip of paper found under the base of the starter for the Blaenau branch stating it had been made at Swindon in 1890. In the end, only the steel post examples were used on the Ffestiniog Railway (at Dduallt) and much of the GWR material ultimately went on to the Severn Valley Railway. The large 'passengers must use the bridge' sign from under the station canopy was also preserved and was affixed on the Ffestiniog's footbridge at Tan-y-Bwlch for many years. Other relics from Bala Junction would see further use on the Llangollen Railway, with the platform edging slabs being recovered for use at Carrog and the preservation era station at Corwen Central.

6
Railway Fundamentals

Tickets

For many prospective passengers arriving at their nearest railway station, the most daunting part of their journey was (and still is) buying their ticket to travel. These were issued by the station staff through a hatch or metal grill inside the station's waiting room or booking hall. Advice on how best to tackle this situation was given in the *Railway Traveller's Handy Book* of 1862:

> All preliminary words are not only a waste of time, but quite unnecessary. The clerk sits at the counter for the purpose of ascertaining the place you are bound for, the class you wish to travel by and the nature of the journey, whether single or double. The readiest way, therefore, of making yourself understood, is to apply for your ticket somewhat after this manner 'Bath—first class—return', or whatever it may be.

This advice did not always save the passenger from falling victim to the humour or sarcasm of the staff on duty. The caustic wit of one of Llangollen's station masters, a Mr Marwood, was well known during the 1890s (from *Llangollen Station: A History* by Paul Lawton):

> Passenger: 'Can you give me an idea of the fare to Torquay?'
> Mr Marwood: 'Did you say idea? Would you rather know the exact fare?'
> Female Passenger: 'Can you tell me the time of the next train to Chester?'
> Mr Marwood: '4.50, Madam.'
> Female Passenger: 'Is there not one before that?'
> Mr Marwood: 'Not before the next, Madam.'
> Passenger: 'Can you give me the time of a through train to Birmingham, please?'
> Mr Marwood: '12.16, Madam'
> Passenger: 'And where do I change?'

Mr Marwood: 'Change what?'
Passenger: 'Where do I change?'
Mr Marwood: 'I think you asked for a through train, Madam'.

The term booking office was adopted from the old coaching practice of issuing tickets from a book. Originally, these tickets on the early railways were handwritten, with the process being both laborious and time-consuming. Its main problem that the ticket-issuing system adopted from the stagecoaches was not designed for handling the large number of passengers that the railways were experiencing. Travelling stagecoaches carried around a dozen passengers, but trains could transport hundreds and the slow ticketing soon caused long impatient queues developing at the country's more popular stations.

The handwritten ticket system also offered unscrupulous station staff an opportunity to defraud the system, by claiming they had sold fewer tickets than they actually had and then pocket the remaining fare money. What was needed was a fast, low-cost, reliable ticket system that could be easily audited and was, therefore, not open to fraud.

The solution came in 1837 from a station master and trained cabinet maker named Thomas Edmondson on the Newcastle and Carlisle railway. The idea was simple enough; sequentially numbered pre-printed tickets made from pasteboard (a stiff type of card), which were date-stamped by a machine upon issue. These Edmondson tickets were a uniform size and shape, meaning that they could be processed by the same machines right the way across the railway network. Their size does not sound particularly standard today—two and a quarter inches long, one and 7/32 of an inch wide and 1/32 of an inch thick—but it worked exceptionally well. This fitted the commercially available pasteboard stock at the time, while being large enough to carry all the pertinent information required.

Each station required its own specially printed stock of tickets to accommodate the wide variety of destinations and classes being offered. For more obscure (or rarely used) destinations, blank tickets (e.g. 'BERWYN to _____') were printed to save space and cope with unforeseen situations. Colour bands, typefaces, and occasionally other graphic images helped staff and passengers to quickly differentiate between the ticket types.

The tickets themselves were kept in a wooden ticket rack within the station's booking office, with the destination and fare being carefully chalked onto a small corresponding label for each ticket type. From the outset, each of the Ruabon to Barmouth line's manned stations issued Edmondson tickets using this standardised system. Where no such facilities existed, such as at Sun Bank Halt and Bonwm Halt, the guard on the train dealt with the issuing of tickets to passengers. In many cases, the guard would issue an 'excess fare' to the next station from where the passenger would then be rebooked to their destination.

However, the system was by no means completely foolproof and on occasions, passengers found ways to get around it. During the 1950s, one ticket that had been issued from London Bridge station for a short, cheap commuter journey to Lee in south-eastern suburbs of the city, was handed in at the station ticket barriers at Leeds, the letters 'DS' having been neatly added to the original destination by the passenger to enable a much longer journey.

Edmondson pasteboard tickets remarkably both pre- and post-dated the Ruabon to Barmouth line, only being replaced after the new APTIS ticketing system (short for advanced passenger ticket information system) was introduced in the 1980s.

Time

With ticket in hand, our prospective Victorian passenger would perhaps like to know what time his train will arrive at its destination. Sitting beside the coal fire in the station's waiting room, listening to the faint ticking of the wall clock, the fundamental information required by our passenger revolves around time.

The early printed timetables were often densely printed and very hard to decipher. Yet, both the timetable and the clock were components of a fundamental and groundbreaking concept that the railways had to invent as they expanded—the concept of standardised time.

Throughout Britain during the early nineteenth century, towns and cities set their clocks to local mean times based on astrological observations. In effect, this meant that noon did not occur at the same time in Penzance as it did in Bristol; in London, there was a two-minute difference between the east and west of the city; and there a full twenty minutes difference between the times in Plymouth and London.

The travelling stagecoaches that predated the railways got around this problem by publishing the corrections needed by travellers for their timepieces *en route*. However, as the railways moved people around the country much more quickly, the whole situation soon became very confusing and needed to be addressed.

In 1840, the Great Western Railway became the first railway to adopt Greenwich Mean Time (GMT). Over the following decade, the other railway companies followed suit. Rather more extraordinarily, so too had 95 per cent of Britain's towns and cities. One after another, they abandoned their own traditional times and moved over to so-called 'railway time'. By 1855, most (though by no means all) public clocks were set to GMT but it was not until 1880 that GMT was officially adopted across the whole of Britain.

One particular legal case in Dorset in 1858 involving a land dispute captured the public's imagination, when a man from Carlisle was late for the hearing and the judge ruled against him. The man protested that he was indeed on time according to his station's clock.

It was all very well having a standardised time system across the Great Western Railway's network, but with a vast array of mechanically operated clocks in use at an ever-increasing number of stations and other premises, it was important for there to be some way of regulating all the clocks on the system. The GWR ultimately adopted the practice that at 10 a.m. every morning, telephones at the principal stations would ring, thus enabling the station staff to correct their clocks accordingly. For all the other stations across the network, it was the station master's job to obtain the precise time form the guard in charge of the first stopping passenger train commencing its journey from a principal station after 10 a.m. If the time given by the guard differed from that of the station clock, the latter was altered to agree accordingly.

Signalling

The safety of passengers has been one of the most important aspects of the line's history since the railway opened. The railway was built initially as just a single line of track, with passing places (loops) along it, enabling two trains to pass each other at these regular intervals. Ensuring that only one train was on each of these single-line sections was of paramount importance, preventing collisions and the ensuing loss of life.

The very earliest railways in Britain were equipped with little in the way of points, junctions, or even many trains. Using a combination of hand-held flags, lamps, pocket watches, messengers and paperwork, the train service was worked using a system of fixed time intervals.

When a train set off along a section of line, a note was made of the time it actually departed. After a fixed period of time (usually ten minutes), another train could depart over the same section of line in the same direction as the first, with the steam locomotive's driver being instructed to proceed with caution. If a longer period of time elapsed, then the driver was informed that he could expect a clear run. Using the flags and lamps, the dispatch of trains could be made more efficient and helped to slightly speed up the system. A little ditty helped railway staff to remember these early signals: 'White is right, Red is wrong, Green is gently go along'.

Gradually, the system developed into using coloured wooden arms on tall signal posts to instruct the locomotive drivers on when they could proceed. The earliest railway signalmen were, in fact, police officers who were employed to keep order on the railway, to set the route along the trackwork and to make sure that the line was clear for the arrival of trains. Indeed, it is still possible to hear signalmen being referred to as 'bobbies' today.

As the complexity of the system increased (including sidings, loops, points, and signals), all the movements of all trains within a local area became controlled from signal boxes at the side of the line. Inside a signal box, the main operating room has a mechanical lever frame in the centre of the floor, with large glazed windows enabling the signalman to see all the train movements outside. Generally, red coloured levers operated all the signals, while the blue and black levers operated the track points. A white coloured lever indicated that this was spare (unused).

All signals and points controlled from the signal box were interlocked to prevent the signalman from setting up two conflicting routes at the same time and to ensure that the signals can be cleared only when the points to which they apply are correctly set. This greatly reduced the risk of trains colliding or derailing. In signal boxes along the line, the interlocking was achieved by tappets and rods mounted beneath the lever frame in the locking room, usually on the ground floor. No two signal boxes controlled exactly the same layout of points and signals, so every locking frame was specially designed and assembled.

Unfortunately, using set time intervals to separate trains had a single major and deadly failing. If a train broke down or encountered any difficulties, there was no way of letting anyone behind know what had happened. On the same section of line, the second train could be bearing down on the stranded train at speed.

The solution came by using a new piece of technology, the electric telegraph. By moving a needle on a dial to point to a certain code or phrase, an electrical message was transmitted along a cable to the next signal box, displaying the same needle position on the receiving dial. Two simple positions for the telegraphic needle could show 'line clear' or 'line blocked'. As a train entered a particular section of track, it ran over a device that sent a single clear message along the cable, causing the needle to display 'line blocked'. It was, therefore, possible to know exactly where a train actually was on the line and the wooden signal arms along the line could be set accordingly.

The block system, as it became known, proved to be a major improvement to safety and in conjunction with the mechanical signal arms, formed the basis of signalling on Britain's railways for over a hundred years. In parallel to the 'block instruments' with their twitching needles, a simple 'bell telegraph' system was used—in essence, a device in a signal box that simply rang a bell in the next signal box along the line. The number of rings on the bell represented a code for certain information. The following basic bell codes and their corresponding meanings are taken from the GWR's regulations book of 1936:

Message being sent:	Beats on bell:
Call Attention	1
'Is Line Clear?' for an Express passenger train	4
'Is Line Clear?' for an Ordinary passenger train	3 pause 1
'Is Line Clear?' for an Auto Train	3 pause 1 pause 3
Train approaching	1 pause 2 pause 1
Train entering section	2
Train out of section	2 pause 1
Stop and examine train	7
Opening signal box	5 pause 5 pause 5
Closing signal box	7 pause 5 pause 5

The telegraph system was a fairly straightforward technology for the railways to install, especially as they already owned the strip of land through which the lines ran. Wooden telegraph poles were erected to carry the wires and became a standard item of lineside equipment across the country. The signalmen in their boxes could now communicate with each other, keeping the trains moving up and down the line while also maintaining a watchful eye on their progress.

Yet, the railways did not operate in splendid isolation to other transportation systems. Where it was not feasible or practicable to construct bridges to carry the railway either over or under roads, level crossings were installed and these had to be linked into the local signalling system.

At Glyndyfrdwy, the line crossed over a minor road immediately to the east of the station platforms and this came under the control of the station's signalman. By turning a large metal wheel within the signal box, the gates could be opened and closed mechanically, although it must be said that the box's position on the platform did give only a restrictive view of the road towards the village.

Where there was not a conveniently placed signal box, other methods of crossing operation had to be implemented. At Llangar Crossing about half a mile west of Corwen, a minor road was crossed near to the ancient Llangar Chapel. The level crossing there was looked after by a crossing keeper, who lived in a small cottage provided by the railway next to it. It was of paramount importance for crossing keepers to know when the next train was approaching and ideally from which direction. Dedicated repeater instruments, consisting of a bell and a telegraphic needle dial, were installed to repeat the information being sent between the nearest signal boxes either side of the crossing (for Llangar, this would have been Corwen West and Llandrillo signal boxes).

The Station Master

The station master was the key authority figure at the railway's stations, being responsible for all station staff working there and instantly recognisable to passengers due to the distinctive uniform worn. Every station master employed by the GWR was also 'answerable for the security and protection of the office and buildings and of the Company's property there'. They were well-respected figures with significant social standing in the local community in which they lived, served, and worked. The complexity of their role varied from station to station, based on the size of the station itself and the number of staff working there.

In its heyday, the GWR regarded Ruabon as an important station, to the extent that the station master's grade there was classed as 'Special Class'. Two platform inspectors were employed to assist with the day-to-day running of the station and at one time, there were sixty staff employed at the station.

With only the one platform and in the absence of any goods facilities, Berwyn was arguably the most basic of the staffed station along the Ruabon to Bala route. It had been constructed for the convenience of the local gentry, being surrounded by the great houses of Plas Berwyn, Plas-yn-Vivod, Llantysilio Hall, and Bryntysilio and was largely operated for their benefit. As a result, the station master at Berwyn had a much closer link with the gentry than would have otherwise been expected.

The author at Berwyn station, 2017.

The chairman of the Llangollen and Corwen Railway, Lt Colonel Charles Tottenham, lived just to the west of the station at Plas Berwyn and through an agreement dating from 1861; he had the right to stop any train passing through Berwyn for his own benefit. At Tottenham's insistence, a first-class waiting room had also been provided at the station in addition to the general waiting room.

It was one of the station master's duties to ensure that passenger trains did stop at Berwyn if and when required by the owner or occupier of Plas Berwyn, or if visitors were expected in advance. To assist with this process, signals and small lever frame on the platform were provided and remained in use until around 1925.

In addition to serving Plas Berwyn, the station master's duties at Berwyn extended out to the other great houses in the locality. For example, when a parcel arrived for the Vivod estate, the station master would display a piece of metal with a large letter 'V' painted on it in one of the upper windows in the station house, so that the butler would know that a package had been delivered which might then be collected by an estate worker.

Fortunately, the details of many of the parcels being received and dispatched from Berwyn in the 1870s have survived, thanks to a remarkable discovery after the station building had closed to the public in the mid-1950s. A cache of GWR way bills (the consignment notes for parcels) was found stored between the rafters in the loft above the station's ticket office. While the handwriting on these is not always easy to decipher, those written in pencil by Mr Roberts in 1874 in particular are still perfectly legible and give a fascinating insight into the parcels being handled in the station during the late Victorian era.

Parcels, cases, sacks, and hampers regularly passed through the station, while two churns came daily from the nearby Llantysilio Farm to be sent off to the Corwen creamery. At the start and end of public school terms, the amount of luggage noticeably increased, with trunks being sent off or collected from Berwyn for the children of the local gentry.

During the summer, a much more unusual delivery was the regular arrival of ice from the Wrexham Lager brewery, which would then be conveyed by barrow down to the Chainbridge Hotel by station staff, ensuring that it was ready in the visitor's room upon their arrival. In the winter months, shot pheasants would be brought down by cart from the Vivod estate and dispatched by train to London for sale the same day. Many of these were destined for hotels in the city, but it is believed that some even ended up on the table of Buckingham Palace.

Yet, the demands of the parcels and passenger traffic at Berwyn were fairly light and afforded the station master plenty of free time to pursue other activities. The station gardens were well looked after, with many of the plants being supplied by the gardeners from the great houses in the locality.

7

Tourism

In the very early days of the line, the Great Western Railway's virtual monopoly over passenger and goods they transported generally dictated the overall advertising policy being used. Small single-sheet handbills were made available from the stations along the line, announcing forthcoming excursions and cheap trips to passengers. Timetable leaflets and books were produced for the regular services, while large posters would be pasted onto boards around the station advertising the GWR's 'special offers' (latest excursions, trips, and new services) and any planned changes to services. After all, the GWR was first and foremost a money-making business and its advertising was an important tool to ensure its profitability.

It was only during the 1890s that the GWR began to exploit the vast possibilities of wider and more subtle forms of advertising, building upon its brand and imagery to tap into new markets. This was mainly with a view to attracting holiday traffic, which grew to become the fundamental source of revenue on the line in later years. New innovations such as pictorial posters, illustrated publications and even guides to holiday accommodation first made their appearance during the 1890s and would be heavily relied upon over the following years.

In effect, the GWR's product that it had to sell was a 40-mile single-track railway, serving four main towns in predominantly rural areas, but passing through superb scenery along its entire length. The original intention to tap into the growing honeypot of the Cambrian Coast had been thwarted by the Cambrian Railway as early as 1868, with the opening of their line from Barmouth Junction to Dolgelly. This short branch made an end-on connection to the GWR's Ruabon to Dolgelly route and despite through ticketing, the GWR was not keen to promote destinations on what was then another company's railway.

Burgeoning traffic demands on the Ruabon to Dolgelly route led to the GWR expending considerable sums of money on new signalling, passing loops, facilities and even the doubling of the section between Ruabon and Llangollen Goods

Junction by 1900. The Great Western Railway (Additional Powers) Act of 1896 had effectively amalgamated all the original railway companies on the Ruabon to Dolgelly route into the GWR, bringing with them the railway's stocks and shares. To ensure that this time, effort and investment had been worthwhile, the GWR pushed on with plans to promote its cross-country route to an even wider audience through some very innovative ideas.

Postcards

Today, picture postcards are to be found in about every tourist shop in North Wales and are very much taken for granted. However, they were first accepted by the Post Office in 1894, when the postage charged for the UK mainland was half a penny. As the writer, R. B. Wilson notes in his book *Go Great Western*:

> The cheap postage and the attraction of the cards themselves led to the very rapid rise of a new industry, and in addition to their use for ordinary messages and greetings, they also provided a new subject for collectors, and in Edwardian times picture postcard collecting became a craze.

The GWR was early on the scene and commissioned its first postcards between 1898 and 1901. Among the general cards produced by The Picture Postcard Co. Ltd in around 1899 were three views around Llangollen ('The Bridge', 'Horse Shoe Falls', and 'Vale Crucis Abbey' [*sic*.]) and two of Dolgelly ('Torrent Walk' and 'Dolgelly and Cader Idris').

Then in March 1904, the GWR issued a set of twenty-five cards printed by R. Tuck and Sons portraying views of its territory. Views from along the Ruabon to Dolgelly line featured on three of this first series: 'The Vale of Llangollen', 'Beautiful Berwyn', and 'Great Western Viaduct, Pontcysyllte near Ruabon'. Two further views along the line—'Pandy Mill near Dolgelly' and 'The Lake at Bala'—were added in a second series in October of that year.

In September and October 1905, another three series of inspiring postcards were released by the GWR, featuring yet more views from along the line. The fourth series featured 'Horseshoe Falls by Great Western Railway to Berwyn', 'Valle Crucis Abbey by Great Western Railway to Berwyn', and 'Footbridge to Old Mill by GWR to Cynwydd [*sic*.]', while the fifth series featured 'On the Tryweryn, Bala' and 'Upper Falls, Dolgelley'.

The postcards were on sale at principal stations and bookstalls across the GWR system and from the beginning were available from automatic machines at some stations, including London Paddington. Indeed, such was the demand when the first series appeared in 1904 that the Paddington machines had to be replenished many times in the first few days.

The popularity of the GWR's publicity postcards began to wane by the end of the First World War and despite their best efforts, a full revival never really took

This picturesque scene of the Dee Gorge entitled 'Beautiful Berwyn' was issued by the GWR in 1904.

GWR postcard: Pandy Mill near Dolgelly.

This 'Valle Crucis Abbey—By Great Western Railway to Berwyn' postcard featured in the GWR's Series 4 and was released in the autumn of 1905.

place. However, their role in publicising the landscape and attractions that were on offer from the GWR's lines cannot be overemphasised and along with other forms of publicity succeeded in boosting passenger numbers on the Ruabon to Dolgelley route during the Edwardian era.

Camping Coaches

In the summer of 1934, the GWR introduced its first camp coaches using withdrawn four- or six-wheel passenger stock. The first season saw coaches deployed at nineteen sites across the GWR system. In their heyday, the camp coaches (or camping coaches as they would later become known) offered holidaymakers the freedom to do as they pleased, in contrast to the regimes of the traditional guest houses and hotels. They also proved to be relatively inexpensive and attractive to families.

The requirement to purchase a given number of railway tickets was not then considered a problem, when many people went on holiday by rail anyway. Holiday cottages and static caravans were virtually unknown and only the relatively rich could afford touring caravans. Camping in tents usually needed a car, especially for families with more than one child, so the camping coach had a virtual monopoly on a corner of the holidaymarket.

The coaches were usually cared for by the station staff, who would clean and service them as part of their normal station duties, although the laundry was often contracted out. Even if the decor and fittings were a bit spartan, it was recognised that they were after all camping coaches by definition and this was to be expected. The coaches were delivered from the GWR's Carriage and Wagon Works at Swindon at the start of each season and returned in the autumn for storage. Four types of coach were available—classified 'A', 'B', 'C', and 'D'—with the difference being in the number of campers that each could accommodate.

For the GWR's centenary year in 1935, the number of sites on offer was doubled from nineteen to thirty-eight. Llangollen was chosen as one of these new sites, but a lack of space around the station area meant that the camp coach had to be located in the sidings at nearby Pentrefelin. This meant that it was about 1 mile from the station and access was via a walk along the canal towpath. A Type 'B' camp coach with six-berth accommodation was allocated to the site between 1935 to 1938, with a Type 'A' coach being allocated for the 1939 season.

Camp coach No. 9985 was the regular coach at Pentrefelin, being noted there during the 1936 and 1937 seasons. It had originally been built as a 31-foot six-wheeled clerestory vehicle by the GWR in February 1884 to diagram U27 (Lot 286) being issued the GWR running number 6245 while in passenger service. It had been condemned in October 1931 and was converted for its new role as a camp coach in June 1934. Internal access throughout the coach was provided, although the placement of the four-berth compartment was less than ideal as the occupants of the two-berth compartment had to pass through the four-berth version in order to reach the living area and kitchen.

Receipts for the 1936 season totalled £6,020, of which £2,481 was from coach rentals and £3,539 from rail train in connection with the bookings.

With the outbreak of war, the weekend of 3 September 1939 proved to be the end of the GWR's camp coach scheme. However, it was quickly realised that the coaches were a very useful resource, with beds as well as washing and cooking facilities; they were ready to serve as mess and sleeping quarters for railway workers and watchers away from home, as well as various military requirements. Pentrefelin regular No. 9985 was noted at Reading in 1942, being used by soldiers assisting with the coaling of the steam locomotives there. By September 1942, it in use with the signal and telegraph department at Reading, with crews being out-stationed in it to undertake repairs at short notice. No. 9985 was condemned (for the second time) in November 1954 and subsequently scrapped.

Following the nationalisation of the 'Big Four' railway companies in 1948, the newly formed British Railways restarted the scheme in 1952. Various methods were used to promote the scheme; regional timetables carrying full-page advertisements, as did their annual 'Holiday Guide'. Several eye-catching posters were also produced for display at stations to capture the imagination. The original stock of camp coaches had in the main had been scrapped and so 'new' coaches were converted from stock dating from the 1901–2 era.

While the pre-war site at Llangollen was not restored, one of the sidings at Carrog station was chosen to host to a camping coach and proved to be very popular. The regular Camping coach there, ex-GWR clerestory bogie coach No.

W9903W, had originally been built back in 1902 to diagram E70 (Lot 986) and then allocated GWR running number 7463. The coach was converted to accommodate eight sleeping berths in 1952. The camping coach at Carrog was made available between March and October each year.

In 1960, the cost of hiring it between June and September was £12 a week, with an additional charge of 17*s* 6*d* being made for the Calor Gas needed for the cooker and lighting inside. One of the conditions of booking was that six adult return rail tickets were purchased from their home station to Carrog (two children counting as one adult). Luggage could be sent in advance and if required, letters could be sent to the station for the holidaymakers. The Carrog station master supervised the arrangements for keys, linen, and crockery among other items, which were dispatched from the stores at Swindon when required.

At the end of the 1962 season, the camping coach was returned to Swindon as usual, after completion of another successful season. However, from 1 January 1963, the London Midland Region of British Rail took over the organisation of the former Western Region lines north of Banbury, including the Ruabon to Barmouth line. This curtailed the camping coach system at Carrog and the facility was not reintroduced.

8
Moving the Goods

When Coal was King

At the time of the Vale of Llangollen Railway's inception, the Great Western Railway was already seeking ways to obtain a regular supply of high quality 'house' coal. The market was booming and at least two rival railway companies—the London and North Western and the Great Northern—were already reaping the rewards of transporting this coal from the north of England to London. The GWR wanted a bigger share of this market.

By 1856, the GWR's attention had turned to a Ruabon colliery which had recently opened but was struggling financially. The colliery was reluctant to shift its limited output away from the profitable local coal market. A dispute between its partners and the resulting court order to dissolve the partnership led the GWR to purchase the colliery's assets.

This situation left the GWR in something of a problem, as it had been established as a railway company, rather than as a colliery owner. The GWR board reached the decision that it was beyond their legal powers to acquire the colliery in their own right but that a separate, nominally independent company could be formed for that purpose.

The Ruabon Coal Company was formed with the GWR's locomotive superintendent, Daniel Gooch, as its chairman. Gooch had joined the GWR back in 1837 after writing to Isambard Kingdom Brunel about the position of the railway's locomotive engineer. Despite Gooch being only twenty years old at the time, Brunel had been so impressed after interviewing him, that he gave him the job at £300 a year. Gooch was later recorded to have said 'I was very young to be entrusted with the management of the locomotive department of so large a railway, but I felt no fear'. He honed his skills on a very steep learning curve and went on to become one of the finest locomotive engineers of the nineteenth century.

With Gooch now holding the positions of GWR locomotive superintendent and the Ruabon Coal Company's chairman, it could be argued that there were

Right: No. 1663 at Ruabon, July 1964.

Below: The wealth of the coalfield around Ruabon proved to be a major boon, particularly to the Great Western Railway. In April 1964, former GWR Hall class 4-6-0 No. 5933 *Kingsway Hall* passes Wynnstay Colliery on the approach to Llangollen Line Junction with a lengthy Up coal train.

distinct conflicts of interest in the way business was conducted. Gooch, along with other GWR employees (including the two sons of the GWR's secretary and the coal manager) used their own capital to form the company. In February 1856, agreements were reached for the company to send a large quantity of coal over the GWR's lines for ten years from January 1857.

These arrangements did not sit well with other colliery owners. In one case, a colliery owner in Lydney in the Forest of Dean took things to court, arguing that the GWR was showing 'undue preference and undue advantage' towards the company. It was true that the Ruabon Coal Company was receiving lower rates and terminal charges for transporting its coal with the GWR, and station agents were allowed commission in order to promote sales of the coal.

However, the Court was of the opinion that because the coal was being transported in bulk, using lengthy and dedicated trains, the lower rate could be justified. The case was dismissed but it only added fuel to the growing consensus that too much power was in the hands of individual GWR executives, without any effective GWR Board control. After all, was it morally right that Gooch should be benefitting financially by doing trade with the company that was paying his salary?

Gooch recognised that he was being cast as a villain and offered to resign either his position as the GWR locomotive superintendent or as chairman of the Ruabon Coal Company if the GWR Board saw that there was a conflict of interest. The offer was dismissed and Gooch continued as locomotive superintendent until September 1864. Upon his retirement from the GWR, Gooch decided to focus his attention on a new attempt to lay a transatlantic cable using Brunel's steamship 'Great Eastern'.

Cattle Class

Before the development of the railways, cattle had to be moved from the local farms to market on foot, which meant that they lost weight and, therefore, their value. The railways brought the opportunity for a much faster, more efficient mechanism for transporting cattle to market and meant that animals could be traded further afield.

Cattle wagons were designed to carry livestock and were commonly attached to goods trains in small numbers. On the former Ruabon to Barmouth line (of which a 10-mile stretch between Llangollen and Corwen has been restored), cattle were taken to market from the smaller stations such as Carrog, with the towns hosting such markets, such as Llangollen, normally having large cattle docks with associated pens. Indeed, when the Llangollen and Corwen Railway opened in 1865, a dedicated cattle train was timetabled to run when required from Corwen, Berwyn, Llangollen, and Ruabon to the Southall market in London.

The movement of cattle was once a regular part of the railway's business and became an integral part in the continued survival of pastoral farming in rural areas. Open upper sides, usually with one or two horizontal iron bars, provided adequate ventilation for the livestock being transported, while openings along the lower sides enabled the muck on the floor to be washed out. A falling access door located centrally on the body sides could fall to form an access ramp.

There were three sizes of GWR wagons for the farmer to choose from depending on the quantity and type of cattle being moved. 'Small' wagons typically had an inside length of 13 feet 6 inches, whereas 'medium' had 15 feet 6 inches and 'large' 18 feet. Both the medium and large variants had moveable internal partitions, meaning that they could have an internal area equal to that of the shorter versions if required.

The surviving GWR livestock rates book from Cynwyd station from the late 1920s gives instructions on which types of livestock could be transported together and which needed to be kept separate. Pigs were not to be loaded into the same vehicle with sheep, calves or goats, unless separated by a moveable partition. Likewise, calves, sheep, goats, or pigs were not to be loaded in with oxen, cows, bulls, horses, or ponies unless properly separated. This did not apply for a cow with its unweaned calf if they were separated from other animals. Small ponies were to be partitioned off and kept separate from horses.

During the late 1920s, livestock from Cynwyd was still being dispatched by rail to destinations right across the railway network, including Manchester, Birmingham, and even the remote Southam Road and Harbury station in Warwickshire.

During the 1930s, there was a switch from transporting livestock to shipping freshly killed meat, which caused a steady reduction in the cattle traffic on the railways. Two of the 'Big Four' railway companies—the LMS and LNER—ceased to build new cattle wagons during the decade. The total national stock had been 19,237 in 1913, 16,150 in 1938, 11,089 at the end of 1948, 6,680 at the end of 1958, and was down to just 4,989 by the start of 1962.

Nonetheless, the numbers of cattle wagons stabilised around 13,000 in the early 1950s, which was actually significantly higher than the 1948 total. The GWR had some on order in 1947 and after nationalisation, Swindon continued to build new cattle wagons until late in 1954. In 1962, British Railways reduced the number of stations open for livestock from over 2,500 to just over 200. This figure dwindled further and by the late 1960s only live cattle being important from Ireland was still being moved by rail. The movement of livestock by rail ceased in 1975.

The double incontinence of the occupants and the consequent frequent washouts led to serious body rot in the lower part of cattle wagons. Consequently, only a handful of vehicles have survived into preservation and the cattle wagon today is a relatively rare sight.

Slate

Mention of slate quarrying and mining within North Wales usually conjures up images from around Snowdonia, including Blaenau Ffestiniog, Penrhyn, and Llanberis among others. Indeed, slate was widely known as 'blue gold' and the finished product from Welsh mines has been used to cover roofs across the globe. Yet, the Dee Valley also had its own share of small but locally important reserves of slate that were to extracted during the early years of the railway. At one stage, three narrow gauge tramways connected slate quarries in the Dee Valley with the GWR's standard gauge line between Ruabon and Corwen.

Glyndyfrdwy's fortunes were transformed by the arrival of the railway and the growth of the slate quarries around it. This boom in slate quarrying around the village during the mid-nineteenth century is exemplified by the Moelferna quarry, which had been just a small exploratory working in the hills to the south of the village before the railway arrived in 1865. It was greatly expanded, with the extracted slate used for slabs, sills, steps, sinks, cisterns, paving, troughs, hospital operating tables, gravestones, billiard tables, and even vat linings for the brewing industry.

In order to transport the slate away from the quarry site, a narrow-gauge tramway was completed in November 1877, linking in with the standard gauge line at an exchange wharf. The following month, the GWR agreed to lay a connecting siding to the east of Glyndyfrdwy station, with the slate being transferred between narrow and standard gauge wagons by means of an overhead gantry crane. This transhipment arrangement was destined to continue well into the 1940s.

Slate has been quarried out around the Llantysilio Mountain and Horseshoe Pass area for several hundred years, with one even dating back to around 1650 and possibly earlier. Production was initially on a limited scale due to land disputes, transportation and lease agreements. In many cases, the costs of transport exceeded that of quarrying the slate, so by the mid-1800s, there was a growing need for a cheap and relianble method of getting the slate down from the quarries to a central processing plant at Pentrefelin, on the outskirts of Llangollen.

Between 1852 and 1857, a 3-foot gauge horse-drawn tramway was constructed, with the 'main' line eventually covering some five miles. Its engineer, Henry Dennis, would later go on to be surveyor and engineer of the nearby Glyn Valley Tramway in Chirk. The tramway connected in with the Llangollen Canal at Pentrefelin, where the slate would have been transferred into awaiting barges for onwards transportation. With the coming of the railway in 1865, a wharf was built for the transfer of slate from the tramway to standard gauge wagons. This opened up new markets for the quarry owners, particularly when a typical canal journey to London could take some three weeks to complete.

The tramway appears to have ceased operating around 1890 and was lifted in 1908. Following closure of the tramway, the slate was transported by lorries from the Oernant Quarry to Llangollen's goods yard for onwards despatch by rail. In their book *Railways of the Dee Valley*, local authors Mark Hambly and Dave Southern noted:

> During 1934 an interesting correspondence took place between the GWR District Goods Manager's Office in Shrewsbury and the Station Master at Llangollen concerning the GWR road lorry based at Llangollen. Apparently the lorry had been having more than its fair share of punctures as a result of being driven over sharp slate waste at the quarry. A representative from the Shrewsbury office visited the quarry and suggested improvements to the loading arrangements to prevent punctures. The improvements were carried out to the satisfaction of the representative and the lorry driver was reminded to exercise care

when visiting the quarry; the closing words of the officer from Shrewsbury being 'otherwise I shall have to consider exchanging the vehicle in question with a solid tyred one'.

Located just over 1 mile west of Carrog station was the aptly named 'Carrog Slate Siding', a private siding maintained by the GWR at the expense of the nearby Penarth Quarry owners. A 2-foot gauge tramway linking the slate workings to the railway system was in use by 1868. The main tramway route encompassed one long incline with a passing loop located at the halfway point. Following the contours of the land meant only shallow cuttings and embankments were required, although a stone-lined tunnel was required to burrow under the Holyhead Road.

In 1868, there were 150 men employed in the Penarth Quarry. The early slate workings were open but soon progressed deeper into the deposits with the digging of adits and levels. By 1883, the number of men employed had reduced to just ten, producing an annual output of around 500 tons. All activity ceased completely by 1890 but over the following years, new investment led to a resurgence in operations. By the 1900s, the output had risen to 1,700 tons.

The GWR's survey in 1924 records that Carrog Slate siding was to be worked from a ground frame, locked by a key on the electric train staff. The GWR working timetable of 1935 provides more detail on the arrangements:

> The points of Carrog Slate Siding are secured by key on the Corwen to Carrog Electric Train Staff. The key of the gates and wheel blocks is kept in a cabin near the Siding points. The Guard is responsible for the whole of the work performed at the Siding and for leaving the facing points, blocks and gates properly secured after the work is completed. Should the Guard find anything wrong at the Siding, or the points, etc. out of order, he must report the matter and defects to the S.M. [station master] at Carrog and also the S.M. at Corwen as soon as he arrives there.

On the Buses

The GWR was a very forward-thinking company and was keen to expand its business wherever possible, even if these were peripheral to its core business of running trains. As early as August 1903, the GWR had commenced a regular bus service in Cornwall, linking the village of Helston with the nearby coastline and beauty spots around Lizard Point. Rather than paying the estimated £85,000 to build a light railway to serve this area, the GWR 'Road Motor Car' services were introduced using two vehicles acquired from the Lynton and Barnstaple Railway in Devon. These proved to be very popular and their introduction took place at a time before any motor buses were running regularly in London.

Intriguingly, the GWR had only just been pipped to the post for launching Britain's very first motor bus service. This had been launched in Eastbourne four months earlier, in April 1903, linking the railway station to the Old Town. The Ilfracombe Motor Coach Company had also already operated railway feeder services on behalf of the narrow-gauge Lynton and Barnstaple Railway, the owner of the former also being the chairman of the latter (the publisher Sir George Newnes).

Further routes were soon established across their network and by 1904, the GWR had thirty-six buses in operation, more than the whole of London. Services started from Wrexham on 11 October of that year, with the routes generally being used as feeders for the trains. Corwen soon developed into a centre for these buses, with routes extending out to Llangollen, Betws-y-Coed, and even Porthmadog on the coast.

Fares			Weekdays*		Sundays
s	d				
			a.m.	p.m.	p.m.
	---	Corwen	9.30	2.20	6.45
	4	Bonwm	9.40	2.30	6.55
	6	Carrog (Station)	9.45	2.35	7.00
	8	Glyn-Dyfrdwy	9.55	2.45	7.10
1	0	Tref-y-Nant	10.05	2.55	7.20
1	2	Berwyn (Station)	10.15	3.05	7.30
1	4	Llangollen	10.30	3.20	7.45
	---	Llangollen	2.00	3.20	7.45
	2	Berwyn (Station)	2.10	3.30	7.55
	6	Tref-y-Nant	2.20	3.40	8.05
	8	Glyn-Dyfrdwy	2.30	3.50	8.15
	10	Carrog (Station)	2.40	4.00	8.25
1	2	Bonwm	2.45	4.05	8.30
1	4	Corwen	3.00	4.20	8.45
* 'Weekdays' was the Victorian term for Monday to Saturday. This service ran on the second and fourth Tuesday in each month only.					

The GWR Road Motor Services timetable from the summer of 1924 gives details on the Llangollen to Corwen and Corwen to Cerrig-y-Druidion routes being operated at that time. The bus service between Llangollen and Corwen railway stations mirrored the course of the railway, even calling at Berwyn and Carrog stations *en route*. The 10-mile journey took an hour to complete and would have cost the prospective passenger 1 shilling and 4 pence each way. Only one weekday round trip operated, with even this being restricted to the second and fourth Tuesday in each month; this increased to two round trips every Sunday.

By comparison, the route out from Corwen Station to the Cerrig-y-Druidion enjoyed a more frequent service due to its importance as a feeder system into the GWR's railway network. Four round trips each weekday were run, departing from Corwen at 6.10 a.m., 10.30 a.m., 1.35 p.m., and 5.15 p.m., and departing from outside the Queen's Hotel in Cerrig-y-Druidion at 7.55 a.m., 11.35 a.m., 3 p.m., and 6.15 p.m.

Children under the age of three were carried for free, while those under twelve were charged approximately half the adult fare. Discounts were also made for block bookings, with books of twenty-four tickets being available for each journey, offering a 12.5 per cent discount on each ticket.

In a sign of the times, the 1924 timetable also records that 'the exterior front seats of closed cars are intended for gentlemen only' and that 'ladies occupying them are charged three pence extra'. This was perhaps a reflection of the wide skirts that were fashionable at the time, taking up more space on the external seats.

The right of a railway company to operate road vehicles was often questioned and as early as 1902 the GWR's solicitor expressed misgivings about the issue. Nonetheless, by the time the Great Western Railway (Road Transport) Act was passed in 1928, the GWR had the largest bus fleet of any British railway company. This paved the way for road services to be transferred out of the railway's control to bus companies. The railway was to remain a shareholder in these companies and efforts would still be made to coordinate bus and rail services.

In 1930, the GWR's bus services in North Wales became part of 'Western Transport', which in turn became amalgamated with the London Midland and Scottish Railway-backed Crosville Motor Services three years later.

Very few details exist on the identity and history of the individual vehicles based at Corwen throughout most of the GWR's ownership. However, some details of the town's allocation between 1927 and 1930 have survived and are detailed below:

Bus No.	Registration No.	Type	Became Lorry	Scrapped
226	E3378	AEC/YB	1927	1932
813	XW1879	Burford 30cwt	09/1928	1933
856	XY2109	Burford 30cwt	1930	1933
865	XY7437	Burford 30cwt	---	Sold 20/7/1931 to Bristol Tramways and Carriage Co.
1546	YV7197	Maudslay ML3		Sold 12/29 to Western Transport
1560	UL8384	Maudslay ML3B	Transferred to Corwen from Weston-super-Mare 05/29	Sold 12/29 to Western Transport
1592	UU4819	Maudslay ML3B	Transferred to Corwen from Cradley Heath 06/1929	Sold 12/29 to Western Transport

Competition from bus services along sections of the route intensified from the 1930s, particularly in and around Llangollen. The 1933 summer timetable for one such competitor, Bryn Melyn Motor Services, shows regular bus services from Llangollen's Town Hall out to Pentredwr (via Valle Crucis Abbey), Rhewl (via Chain Bridge and Llantysilio), and a Wednesday-only service to Oswestry. There is even a Sunday-only service listed from Llangollen to Llantysilio Church near Berwyn to assist worshippers attending the evening service there; the special return fare was 6d.

As an interesting aside, during the early Edwardian era, there was a proposal to build an electric tramway linking Llangollen and Valle Crucis Abbey, although nothing ever came of the scheme. The *North Wales Chronicle* of 11 January 1902 reported:

> A syndicate has been formed for the purpose of constructing electric cars to run between Llangollen and Valle Crucis Abbey. Last summer several Americans were at Llangollen and it is believed that the proposed system is the outcome of the visit. The Americans also approached several of the proprietors of the flannel factories about Llangollen and Glyn with a view of purchasing the factories, but no agreement or sale has yet been affected.

Bryn Melyn motor services timetable around Llangollen, 1933.

Rhosymedre Bridge was the first road overbridge from Llangollen Line Junction. It takes the form of a 27-foot-6-inch-wide arch constructed of local stone. Today, the old trackbed is an access road to the Cefn Druids Football Club's aptly named Rock Stadium.

One of the more unusual bridges on the line was the narrow stone subway at Australia, just to the west of Trevor station. The name was derived from the nearby Trevor silica brickworks, which was also known as the Australia brickworks, and was operational by 1885.

Bryn Howel Canal Bridge, 2011.

The Canal Bridge at 3 miles 10 chains is perhaps the most known due to its prominent position spanning the Llangollen Canal. The original stone piers received blue engineering brick during subsequent repairs and strengthening work, while the concrete deck is believed to date from the 1950s.

Cattle Arch near Sun Bank Halt.

Bridge 28 near Bonwm, 2014.

Above and below: Dee Bridge near Pentrefelin, October 2015.

List of Bridges and Culverts on the Ruabon to Llandrillo Section

(Mileage Given from Llangollen Line Junction)

NAME	MILEAGE	SIZE	DESCRIPTION	REMARKS
Rhosymedre	0 m 40 ch	11 feet 9 inches sq. span	Road under	Girder bridge with skew span of 17 feet 6 inches and height of 12 feet 3 inches.
Rhosymedre	0 m 46 ch	27 feet 6 inches sq. span	Road over	Stone arch, 18 feet 6 inches height.
Coed Richard Footbridge	0 m 54 ch	40 feet sq. span.	Footpath over	Timber footbridge, 58 feet height.
Over Footpath and Pontcysyllte Line	0 m 63 ch	11 feet 9 inches and 25 feet sq. spans	Rail over rail	Stone bridges over private footpath and Pontcysyllte branch
Llangollen Road	1 m 04 ch	39 feet 6 inches sq. span	Road under	Stone arch with 44 feet skew span, 23 feet 6 inches height.
Trefnant	1 m 30 ch		Road under	
Parry's Farm	1 m 35 ch		Road over	
Parry's Farm	1 m 55 ch		Road over	Stone arch
Llangollen Road	1 m 60 ch	27 feet 9 inches sq. span	Road over	Stone arch with 39 feet skew span, 15 feet 9 inches height.
Subway (Australia)	2 m 02 ch		Farm track underpass	Stone arch
Plasynpentre	2 m 27 ch	24 feet 10 inches to 25 feet span	Road under	Stone arch, metal railings. Arch height 14 feet above road level.
Llyn Farm	2 m 47 ch		Farm track underpass	Concrete span, metal railings
Bryn Howell	2 m 78 ch		Road over	Stone skew arch
Canal Bridge	3 m 10 ch	22 feet 2 inches between abutments	Canal under	Concrete skew span, metal railings. Canal bridge No. 39W.
Bryn Howell	3 m 18 ch	25 feet 5 inches span	Road under	Stone arch, metal railings
Cattle Arch	3 m 40 ch		Farm track underpass	Iron girder span
Subway (Woodlands)	5 m 05 ch		Footpath under	
Subway (Factory Crossing)	5 m 18 ch		Footpath under	
Bowling Green Footbridge	5 m 20 ch		Footpath over	
Main Road (Bishop Trevor)	5 m 33 ch	26 feet square span	Road over	14 feet height
Green Lane	5 m 45 ch		Track over	Stone arch
Jenny Jones	5 m 61 ch		Farm track underpass	Iron girder span
Glandwr	5 m 67 ch		Farm track underpass	Iron girder span
Cattle Creep	6 m 15 ch		Farm track underpass	Iron girder span

NAME	MILEAGE	SIZE	DESCRIPTION	REMARKS
River Dee	6 m 36 ch		River underpass	Three metal skew spans
Subway	7 m 01 ch	6 feet span	Footpath underpass	Iron girder span. WW1 soldiers pencil messages present on glazed white tiles.
Berwyn Viaduct (King's Bridge)	7 m 05 ch (7 m 06 ch)	-	Road and stream underpass	Six stone and brick spans were each between 29 feet 3 inches and 30 feet 3 inches wide, crossing the Eirianallt stream at a height of 36 feet 6 inches.
Rhysgog Bridge	7 m 10 ch		Road over	Iron girder span
Berwyn Tunnel	7 m 55 ch	689 yards in length		
Deeside	8 m 50 ch		Farm track underpass	Iron girder span
Garthdwr	9 m 43 ch		Farm track underpass	Iron girder span
Cattle Creep	10 m 0 ch			Iron girder span
Cattle Creep	10 m 10 ch			Iron girder span
Cattle Creep	10 m 72 ch			Iron girder span
Cattle Creep	11 m 48 ch			Iron girder span
Main Road (Carrog)	12 m 70 ch		Road over	Stone arch
Cattle Creep	13 m 57 ch			Iron girder span
Cattle Creep	14 m 02 ch			
Cattle Creep	14 m 30 ch			Iron girder span
Ty Isaf	14 m 60 ch		Access road over	Stone arch
Ty Isaf	15 m 02 ch		Farm track underpass	Stone arch
Ty Isaf	15 m 18 ch		Farm track underpass	Iron girder span
Ty Isaf	15 m 22 ch		Farm track underpass	Iron girder span
Tyn Ddol	15 m 30 ch		Road under	
Holyhead Road	16 m 00 ch		Road over	Iron girder span. Stone abutments.
Cattle Creep	17 m 01 ch			
Cynwyd	17 m 54 ch		Road over	Iron girder span. Stone abutments.
Cynwyd Brook	17 m 66 ch			
Cattle Creep	18 m 03 ch			
Cattle Creep	18 m 31 ch			
To Hendwr Field	19 m 41 ch		Brook underpass	24 feet 11.75 inches iron girder span crossing the Glyn Brook
Cattle Arch	19 m 55 ch			

Bibliography

Baughn, P. E., *A Regional History of the Railways of Great Briatin, Vol. 11: North and Mid Wales* (David and Charles, 1980)

Dickinson, P., *Steam in the Dee Valley: From Ruabon to Corwen via Llangollen* (published privately, 2015)

Fenton, M., *Camp Coach Holidays on the GWR* (Wild Swan Publications, 1999)

Iorweth Roberts, J., *Early Railways Controversies at Llangollen* (Denbighshire Historical Society, 1960)

Kitchenside, G. M. and Williams, A., *British Railways Signalling* (Fourth Edition) (Ian Allen Ltd, 1978)

Lawton, P., *Carrog: A Welsh Country Station* (A Purely Local Publiation)

Mitchell, V. and Smith, K., *Western Main Lines: Ruabon to Barmouth featuring Llangollen* (Middleton Press, 2010)

Rear, W. G. and Jones, N., *The Llangollen Line: Ruabon to Barmouth* (Book Law Publications, 2012)

Thomas, J. R. and Southern, D. W., *The Industrial Tramways of the Vale of Llangollen* (The Oakwood Press)

Williams, M. F., *The Ruabon to Barmouth Line: Reflections of a Lost Welsh Railway* (Lightmoor Press, 2015)

Wilson, R. B., *Go Great Western: A History of GWR Publicity* (David St John Thomas, 1987)